InDesign CS5: Basic

Student Manual

ACE Edition

InDesign CS5: Basic, ACE Edition

President, Axzo Press:	Jon Winder
Vice President, Product Development:	Charles G. Blum
Vice President, Operations:	Josh Pincus
Director of Publishing Systems Development:	Dan Quackenbush
Writer:	Jim O'Shea
Copyeditor:	Catherine Oliver
Keytester:	Cliff Coryea

Trademarks

ILT Series is a trademark of Axzo Press.

Some of the product names and company names used in this book have been used for identification purposes only and may be trademarks or registered trademarks of their respective manufacturers and sellers.

Disclaimers

We reserve the right to revise this publication and make changes from time to time in its content without notice.

The Adobe Approved Certification Courseware logo is either a registered trademark or trademark of Adobe Systems Incorporated in the United States and/or other countries. The Adobe Approved Certification Courseware logo is a proprietary trademark of Adobe. All rights reserved.

The ILT Series is independent from ProCert Labs, LLC and Adobe Systems Incorporated, and are not affiliated with ProCert Labs and Adobe in any manner. This publication may assist students to prepare for an Adobe Certified Expert exam, however, neither ProCert Labs nor Adobe warrant that use of this material will ensure success in connection with any exam.

Student Manual
ISBN 10: 1-4260-2093-7
ISBN 13: 978-1-4260-2093-3

Student Manual with Disc
ISBN-10: 1-4260-2095-3
ISBN-13: 978-1-4260-2095-7

Printed in the United States of America
2 3 4 5 6 GL 14 13 12 11

Contents

Introduction

After reading this introduction, you will know how to:

A Use ILT Series manuals in general.

B Use prerequisites, a target student description, course objectives, and a skills inventory to properly set your expectations for the course.

C Re-key this course after class.

Topic A: About the manual

ILT Series philosophy

Our manuals facilitate your learning by providing structured interaction with the software itself. While we provide text to explain difficult concepts, the hands-on activities are the focus of our courses. By paying close attention as your instructor leads you through these activities, you will learn the skills and concepts effectively.

We believe strongly in the instructor-led class. During class, focus on your instructor. Our manuals are designed and written to facilitate your interaction with your instructor, and not to call attention to manuals themselves.

We believe in the basic approach of setting expectations, delivering instruction, and providing summary and review afterwards. For this reason, lessons begin with objectives and end with summaries. We also provide overall course objectives and a course summary to provide both an introduction to and closure on the entire course.

Manual components

The manuals contain these major components:

- Table of contents
- Introduction
- Units
- Course summary
- Glossary
- Index

Each element is described below.

Table of contents

The table of contents acts as a learning roadmap.

Introduction

The introduction contains information about our training philosophy and our manual components, features, and conventions. It contains target student, prerequisite, objective, and setup information for the specific course.

Units

Units are the largest structural component of the course content. A unit begins with a title page that lists objectives for each major subdivision, or topic, within the unit. Within each topic, conceptual and explanatory information alternates with hands-on activities. Units conclude with a summary comprising one paragraph for each topic, and an independent practice activity that gives you an opportunity to practice the skills you've learned.

The conceptual information takes the form of text paragraphs, exhibits, lists, and tables. The activities are structured in two columns, one telling you what to do, the other providing explanations, descriptions, and graphics.

Course summary

This section provides a text summary of the entire course. It is useful for providing closure at the end of the course. The course summary also indicates the next course in this series, if there is one, and lists additional resources you might find useful as you continue to learn about the software.

Glossary

The glossary provides definitions for all of the key terms used in this course.

Index

The index at the end of this manual makes it easy for you to find information about a particular software component, feature, or concept.

Manual conventions

We've tried to keep the number of elements and the types of formatting to a minimum in the manuals. This aids in clarity and makes the manuals more classically elegant looking. But there are some conventions and icons you should know about.

Item	Description
Italic text	In conceptual text, indicates a new term or feature.
Bold text	In unit summaries, indicates a key term or concept. In an independent practice activity, indicates an explicit item that you select, choose, or type.
`Code font`	Indicates code or syntax.
`Longer strings of ▶` `code will look ▶` `like this.`	In the hands-on activities, any code that's too long to fit on a single line is divided into segments by one or more continuation characters (▶). This code should be entered as a continuous string of text.
Select **bold item**	In the left column of hands-on activities, bold sans-serif text indicates an explicit item that you select, choose, or type.
Keycaps like ↵ ENTER	Indicate a key on the keyboard you must press.

Hands-on activities

The hands-on activities are the most important parts of our manuals. They are divided into two primary columns. The "Here's how" column gives short instructions to you about what to do. The "Here's why" column provides explanations, graphics, and clarifications. Here's a sample:

Do it!

A-1:   Creating a commission formula

Here's how	Here's why
1 Open Sales	This is an oversimplified sales compensation worksheet. It shows sales totals, commissions, and incentives for five sales reps.
2 Observe the contents of cell F4	F4 ▼ = =E4*C_Rate
	The commission rate formulas use the name "C_Rate" instead of a value for the commission rate.

For these activities, we have provided a collection of data files designed to help you learn each skill in a real-world business context. As you work through the activities, you will modify and update these files. Of course, you might make a mistake and therefore want to re-key the activity starting from scratch. To make it easy to start over, you will rename each data file at the end of the first activity in which the file is modified. Our convention for renaming files is to add the word "My" to the beginning of the file name. In the above activity, for example, a file called "Sales" is being used for the first time. At the end of this activity, you would save the file as "My sales," thus leaving the "Sales" file unchanged. If you make a mistake, you can start over using the original "Sales" file.

In some activities, however, it might not be practical to rename the data file. If you want to retry one of these activities, ask your instructor for a fresh copy of the original data file.

Topic B: Setting your expectations

Properly setting your expectations is essential to your success. This topic will help you do that by providing:

- Prerequisites for this course
- A description of the target student
- A list of the objectives for the course
- A skills assessment for the course

Course prerequisites

Before taking this course, you should be familiar with personal computers and the use of a keyboard and a mouse. Furthermore, this course assumes that you've completed the following courses or have equivalent experience:

- *Windows 7: Basic*

Target student

This course is designed for students who want to use Adobe InDesign to create professional documents and print layouts. You should have little or no experience using Adobe InDesign, but experience using a word processing application is recommended. You will get the most out of this course if your goal is to learn how to use Adobe InDesign CS5 to create professional print documents and publications.

Adobe ACE certification

This course is also designed to help you pass the Adobe Certified Expert (ACE) exam for InDesign CS5. For complete certification training, you should complete this course and both of the following:

- *InDesign CS5: Advanced, ACE Edition*
- *InDesign CS5: Production, ACE Edition*

Course objectives

These overall course objectives will give you an idea about what to expect from the course. It is also possible that they will help you see that this course is not the right one for you. If you think you either lack the prerequisite knowledge or already know most of the subject matter to be covered, you should let your instructor know that you think you are misplaced in the class.

Note: In addition to the general objectives listed below, specific ACE exam objectives are listed at the beginning of each topic (where applicable).

After completing this course, you will know how to:

- Start Adobe InDesign, explore elements of the environment, set preferences and defaults, and use Adobe Community Help.

- Create documents and document presets; create and place text; place graphics and other InDesign pages; and work with color swatches.

- Position elements precisely by using guides and the Control panel; and use master pages.

- Thread text between text frames, add jump lines, and use columns in text frames; use the Paragraph Formatting controls; use Find/Change to replace formatting; and create and edit paragraph and character styles.

- Position text in text frames and format frame edges; place Photoshop images in documents, set text wrap, modify graphics, and nest frames; group objects and manipulate objects within a group; and create layers and assign objects to them.

- Print documents, create print presets, and export documents to PDF; and prepare documents for commercial printing.

Skills inventory

Use the following form to gauge your skill level entering the class. For each skill listed, rate your familiarity from 1 to 5, with five being the most familiar. *This is not a test*. Rather, it is intended to provide you with an idea of where you're starting from at the beginning of class. If you're wholly unfamiliar with all the skills, you might not be ready for the class. If you think you already understand all of the skills, you might need to move on to the next course in the series. In either case, you should let your instructor know as soon as possible.

Skill	1	2	3	4	5
Starting InDesign and customizing the workspace					
Navigating in documents					
Examining basic panels					
Setting preferences					
Using Adobe Community Help					
Creating documents					
Creating text in a document					
Placing text					
Placing graphics					
Placing InDesign pages					
Creating custom color swatches					
Loading and saving swatches					
Aligning elements to guides					
Positioning elements by using the Control panel					
Using smart guides					
Using master pages					
Overriding a master-page object on a document page					
Threading text					
Adding columns to text frames					
Adding jump-line page numbers					
Setting keep options					
Creating bulleted and numbered lists					

Skill	1	2	3	4	5
Creating drop caps					
Adjusting the spacing between paragraphs					
Creating paragraph rules					
Using Find/Change					
Creating, editing, and applying styles					
Positioning text in a text frame					
Formatting a frame edge					
Placing Photoshop files					
Setting text wrap					
Modifying graphics					
Nesting frames					
Grouping objects and manipulating objects in groups					
Creating layers and assigning objects to layers					
Changing the layer stacking order					
Printing a proof of a document					
Exporting a document as a PDF					
Checking spelling					
Checking fonts and linked graphics in a document					
Preflighting a document					
Packaging a publication					

Topic C: Re-keying the course

If you have the proper hardware and software, you can re-key this course after class. This section explains what you'll need in order to do so, and how to do it.

Hardware requirements

Your personal computer should have:

- A keyboard and a mouse
- Intel Pentium 4 or AMD Athlon 64 Processor (or faster)
- 1GB RAM (or higher)
- At least 2 GB of hard-disk space
- A DVD-ROM drive for installation
- A monitor with at least 1280×960 resolution at 24-bit color or better

Software requirements

You will also need the following software:

- Microsoft Windows 7 (You can also use Windows Vista or Windows XP, but the screen shots in this course were taken in Windows 7, so your screens might look somewhat different.)
- Adobe InDesign CS5
- Adobe Reader (If this is not installed, you will not be able to complete Activity A-2 in the unit titled "Finalizing documents.")
- The HP LaserJet 5200 Series PCL 5 printer driver (An actual printer is not required, but without this printer driver, you will not be able to complete Activity A-1, in the unit titled "Finalizing documents," as written.)

Network requirements

The following network components and connectivity are also required for re-keying this course:

- Internet access, for the following purposes:
  - Downloading the latest critical updates and service packs
  - Completing Activity C-1 in the unit titled "Getting started"
  - Downloading the Student Data files (if necessary)
- Activating InDesign CS5

Setup instructions to re-key the course

Before you re-key the course, you will need to perform the following steps.

1   Use Windows Update to install all available critical updates and service packs.

2   With flat-panel displays, we recommend using the panel's native resolution for best results. Color depth/quality should be set to High (24 bit) or higher.

    Please note that your display settings or resolution may differ from the author's, so your screens might not exactly match the screenshots in this manual.

3   If necessary, reset any InDesign CS5 defaults that you have changed. If you do not wish to reset the defaults, you can still re-key the course, but some activities might not work exactly as documented.

    a   Press and hold Shift+Ctrl+Alt and start InDesign. Pressing Shift+Ctrl+Alt as InDesign starts causes a dialog box to appear, in which you can specify to delete the InDesign Preference file. Click Yes to delete the file.

    b   In InDesign, from the Workspace menu, choose Delete Workspace. In the Delete Workspace dialog box, select All from the Name list and click Delete. Click Yes to delete all of the custom workspaces.

    c   Close InDesign.

4   If you have the data disc that came with this manual, locate the Student Data folder on it and copy it to your Windows desktop.

    If you don't have the data disc, you can download the Student Data files for the course:

    a   Connect to www.axzopress.com.

    b   Under Downloads, click Instructor-Led Training.

    c   Browse the subject categories to locate your course. Then click the course title to display a list of available downloads. (You can also access these downloads through our Catalog listings.)

    d   Click the link(s) for downloading the Student Data files.

    e   Create a folder named Student Data on your Windows desktop.

    f   Double-click the downloaded zip file(s) and drag the contents into the Student Data folder.

CertBlaster software

CertBlaster pre- and post-assessment software is available for this course. To download and install this free software, complete the following steps:

1   Go to www.axzopress.com.

2   Under Downloads, click CertBlaster.

3   Click the link for InDesign CS5: Basic, ACE Edition.

4   Save the .EXE file to a folder on your hard drive. (**Note:** If you skip this step, the CertBlaster software will not install correctly.)

5   Click Start and choose Run.

6   Click Browse and navigate to the folder that contains the .EXE file.

7   Select the .EXE file and click Open.

8   Click OK and follow the on-screen instructions. When prompted for the password, enter **c_indescs5**.

Unit 1

Getting started

Unit time: 30 minutes

Complete this unit, and you'll know how to:

A Start Adobe InDesign and explore elements of the environment.

B Set preferences and defaults.

C Use the InDesign Support Center Web site to get InDesign help.

Topic A: The Adobe InDesign environment

Explanation

The world of professional desktop publishing is dominated by two programs: Adobe InDesign and QuarkXPress. Designers increasingly are drawn to InDesign for (among other reasons) its integration with Adobe's other Creative Suite programs, including Photoshop, Flash, and Dreamweaver. InDesign remains primarily a program for producing print publications, ranging from one-page flyers to magazines and books. But as the definition of *desktop publishing* expands beyond layouts produced on personal computers for print media to include content for online use and for portable electronic devices, the features of InDesign have expanded to include support for a variety of publishing media.

The InDesign workspace

You start InDesign by clicking Start and choosing All Programs, Adobe InDesign CS5. The InDesign Welcome screen appears by default. From here, you can open recent documents, create documents, or access online community features. (You can open the Welcome screen at any time by choosing Help, Welcome Screen.)

To open a document, choose File, Open. Navigate to the desired folder, select the InDesign file you want to open, and click Open.

To close a document, choose File, Close or click the Close button in the upper-right corner of the document window. (You can also press Ctrl+W.) If you've changed the document, a dialog box appears, prompting you to save the changes before closing. Click Yes to save the changes and close the document.

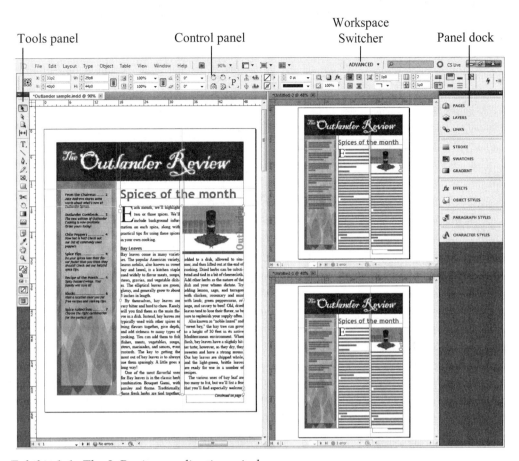

Exhibit 1-1: The InDesign application window

Panels and docks

The application window, shown in Exhibit 1-1, includes panels that, by default, appear on the right side of the window as icon groups. To view a panel, click the icon. To close a panel, click the icon again.

Click the Expand Panels icon at the top of the panel dock to show one panel from each panel group, as shown in Exhibit 1-2. You can then click the Collapse to Icons button to return the docked panels to button form. If you need more space in the application window, you can drag the edge of the dock to the right until only the icon is displayed. To display or hide a docked panel, click its name or its icon.

You can display panels that are not already visible in the dock by choosing them from the Window menu. They appear as floating panels. For example, to display the Text Wrap panel, choose Window, Text Wrap. If a panel is already displayed, then choosing it from the Window menu will hide it.

To dock a floating panel, drag its tab (where the panel name is displayed) to the left or right edge of the application window. Similarly, to convert a docked panel to a floating panel, drag its tab away from its panel group. You can arrange panels into groups by dragging them to existing groups or by dragging them to another panel to create a new group. You can create multiple panel docks by dragging window tabs to either the left or right edge of an existing dock.

You cannot put the Tools panel or the Control panel into docked groups, but you can convert them to floating panels and dock them individually. You can dock the Control panel at the top or bottom of the application window, and you can dock the Tools panel on the left or right edges of the application window.

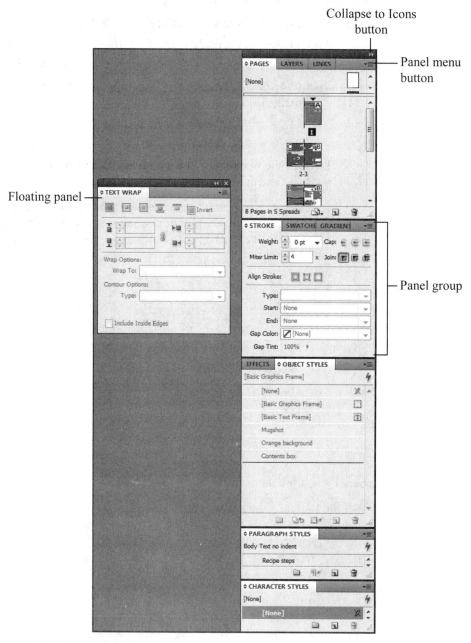

Exhibit 1-2: Various panel configurations

Workspaces

As you work on various projects, you might find that you're opening and closing various panels and arranging them in different configurations. InDesign's workspace settings display panels appropriate for different tasks, and you can configure and save your own custom workspaces.

To create and save a custom workspace:

1   Arrange the panels as desired.

2   From the Workspace Switcher menu, choose New Workspace.

3   In the New Workspace dialog box, in the Name box, enter a name for the workspace.

4   Under Capture, check the desired options.

5   Click OK.

6   To open the workspace you've saved, choose its name from the Workspace Switcher menu.

You can always reset any workspace to the default configuration. For example, you might open the Advanced workspace and rearrange some of the panels. To reset the panels to their defaults, choose Reset Advanced from the Workspace Switcher menu.

A-1:   Starting InDesign and customizing the workspace

The files for this activity are in Student Data folder **Unit 1\Topic A**.

Here's how	Here's why
1 Click **Start** and choose **All Programs**, **Adobe InDesign CS5**	To open the application window. The Welcome screen appears.
Check **Don't show again**	(In the lower-left corner of the Welcome screen.) To see this screen in the future, choose Help, Welcome Screen.
Close the Welcome screen	
2 Observe the application window	The Control panel, the Tools panel, and panel icons in the panel dock are visible.
3 Choose **File**, **Open...**	To open the Open a File dialog box.
4 Navigate to the current topic folder	In the current unit folder.
Select the file **Outlander Sample**	
Click **Open**	A warning box might appear, stating that links in the file need to be updated. This occurs because Windows gives files new "created" or "modified" dates when files are copied from one computer to another, and InDesign treats the files as if they have been modified.
Click **Update Links**	
5 Above the Control panel, click as shown	To display the Screen Mode flyout menu.
Choose **Preview**	To show the document in Preview mode. You see the document as it will look when printed.
Display the Screen Mode flyout menu and choose **Normal**	To return to Normal view.
6 Click the Workspace Switcher button and choose **New in CS5**	To change the set of panels displayed in the dock.

7 In the panel dock, click the Pages icon

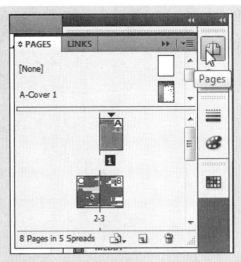

To show the Pages panel.

Drag the Pages panel tab away from the panel group, as shown

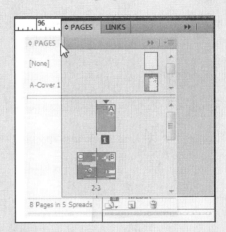

To make it a floating panel.

8 Choose **Window**, **Text Wrap**

To open the Text Wrap panel.

9 From the Workspace Switcher menu, choose **New Workspace...**

To open the New Workspace dialog box.

Edit the Name box to read **My workspace**

Under Capture, verify that **Panel Locations** is checked, and click **OK**

To save the workspace. The name of the custom workspace appears on the Workspace Switcher button.

10 From the Workspace Switcher menu, choose **New in CS5**

InDesign automatically saved the changes you made in this default workspace. You'll reset the default locations of the panels.

From the Workspace Switcher menu, choose **Reset New in CS5**

To return to the defaults for this workspace.

11 From the Workspace Switcher menu, choose **Advanced**

To use the Advanced workspace.

Elements of an InDesign document

Explanation

An InDesign document can contain up to 9,999 pages. Most documents you work with, of course, will contain far fewer pages than that.

When you open a document, you'll see the document window, as shown in Exhibit 1-3. It contains the document you're working with, as well as a pasteboard area. Ruler guides at the top and left of the document window help you arrange elements on the page. The status bar shows the current page number and the Live Preflight status.

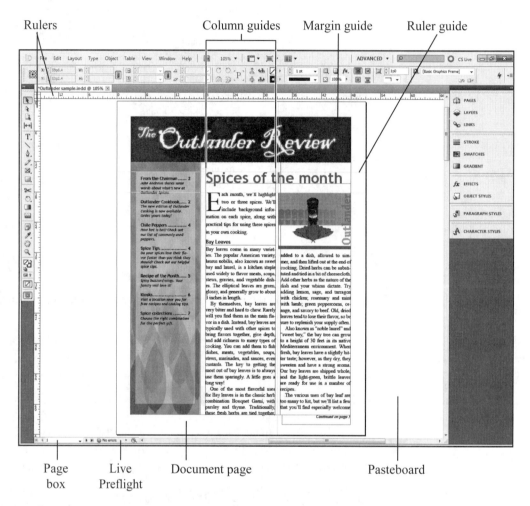

Exhibit 1-3: An InDesign document window

The following table describes some of the elements of the document window.

Element	Description
Rulers	The document window contains horizontal and vertical rulers, which you can use to position items. As you move items in a document, the rulers indicate the item's position. By default, both rulers use picas, but you can set them to other units of measure.
Column guides	These guides (indicated by violet lines) show where columns are located on a page.
Margin guides	These guides (indicated by magenta lines inside the page boundaries) show where margins are located on a page. By default, margin guides are visible on every page of a document. Margin guides and other types of InDesign guides don't print.

Element	Description
Ruler guides	These are guides you add to make it easier to position items. Ruler guides can be horizontal or vertical, and they do not print. There are two types of ruler guides: *page guides*, which appear on a single page, and *spread guides*, which appear across all pages of a spread as well as on the pasteboard.
Live Preflight	By checking the Live Preflight status, you can immediately see whether your document contains any errors that would cause a problem in the production stage.
Pasteboard	This is the blank area that surrounds document pages. You can store text and graphics on the pasteboard until you are ready to use them. Items on the pasteboard do not print, but they are saved with the document. Each page or spread has its own pasteboard.
Document page	This is where you create the layout for your publication. Items inside the page boundaries (indicated by black lines) will print when you print the publication.

Navigation

Before you can work in a document, you need to know how to move between pages and zoom in and out. You'll often need to alternate between zooming in closely to see details and zooming out to see how elements look in an entire spread.

Moving between pages in a document

There are several ways to move between pages in a document:

- Double-click a page thumbnail in the Pages panel. The highlighted page icon indicates which page you're viewing.

- In the status bar, enter a page number in the page box and press Enter. This method is useful if you have a document with many pages.

- In the status bar, select a page from the page list (to the right of the page box).

- Hold Spacebar to temporarily select the Hand tool, and then drag in the document window. While using the Hand tool, you can access the Zoom tool— hold Ctrl+Spacebar to zoom in, and hold Ctrl+Alt+Spacebar to zoom out. (Note, however, that pressing shortcut keys when the insertion point is in a text frame will insert text.) You can also press H to switch to the Hand tool.

- Press Page Down or Page Up to scroll through the document. You can also press Alt+Page Down or Alt+Page Up to move to the next or previous spread. Press Shift+Page Down or Shift+Page Up to move to the next or previous page.

- Choose an option from the Layout menu. You can choose First Page, Previous Page, Next Page, Last Page, Next Spread, Previous Spread, Go To Page, Go Back, or Go Forward.

Zooming

You can zoom in and out to work with page items more easily. There are different methods of zooming. The most appropriate method to use depends on what you are trying to see.

- Press Ctrl+= or Ctrl+– to zoom in or out. If an object is selected, InDesign will center on that object while zooming. Otherwise, zooming will center on the current page or spread.

- Press Ctrl+1 to view a page at actual size. The "actual size" of your document displayed on the screen depends on several factors but usually doesn't result in displaying your document at actual size.

- Press Ctrl+2 to view a page at 200%.

- Press Ctrl+0 to fit the entire page in the document window.

- Press Alt+Ctrl+0 to fit the entire spread in the document window.

- Press Ctrl+Spacebar or Ctrl+Alt+Spacebar to temporarily access the Zoom tool and zoom in or out.

- Using the Zoom tool, drag in the document window to zoom in on a portion of a page. This method is useful for zooming in on small items.

- Using the Zoom tool, click in the document window to zoom in incrementally on a section of a page. You can also press Alt and click to zoom out.

- From the Zoom Level menu, choose a zoom percentage. You can also enter a percentage in the Zoom level box.

Another method of zooming, called *power zoom*, involves using the Hand tool. With the Hand tool selected, point to an area of the document and press and hold the mouse button. After a few seconds, InDesign zooms to show the entire pasteboard in the document window, as shown in Exhibit 1-4. While holding the mouse button, drag to move to different areas of the document. Press Up Arrow or Down Arrow to reduce or increase the focus area, indicated by a red border. When you've moved the border to the desired area, release the mouse button to zoom. If you haven't adjusted the focus area, InDesign zooms to the previous zoom level; otherwise, it zooms to fill the focus area you've specified.

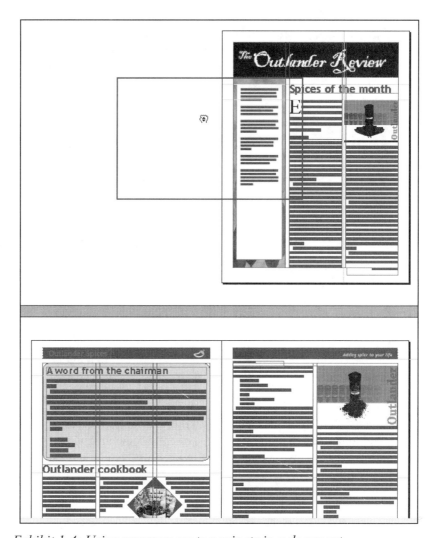

Exhibit 1-4: Using power zoom to navigate in a document

Multiple document windows

You can have multiple documents open at once. Each new document you open appears on a new tab, as shown in Exhibit 1-1. When you have more than one document open, you can select different views to see them all at once. To do so, click the Arrange Documents button, shown in Exhibit 1-5, and choose an option from the menu. (The buttons shown in Exhibit 1-5 are located to the right of the menu bar.)

These views are referred to as *N-up views*, where N is the number of windows arranged in the view option. You can choose Float All in Windows from the Arrange Documents menu to show each document in its own separate document window. In addition, you can drag the documents' tabs to arrange them in the application window.

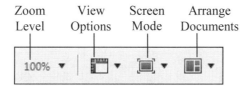

Exhibit 1-5: Options for viewing document windows

Do it!

A-2: Navigating a document

Here's how	Here's why

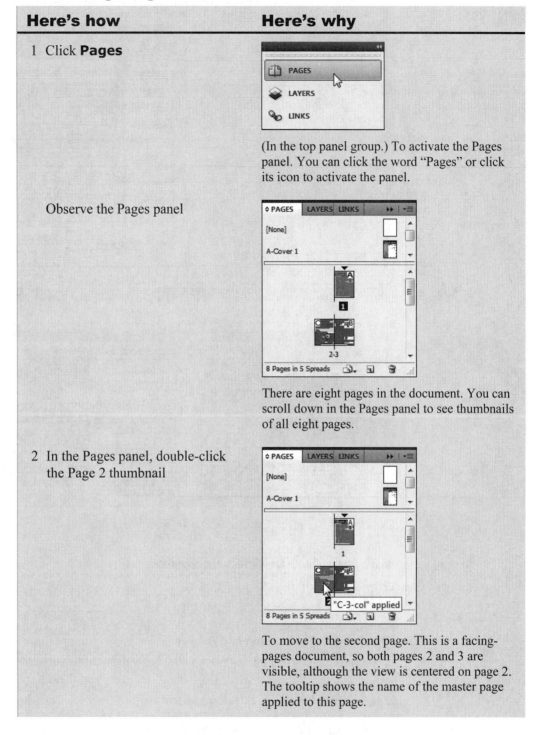

1 Click **Pages**

(In the top panel group.) To activate the Pages panel. You can click the word "Pages" or click its icon to activate the panel.

Observe the Pages panel

There are eight pages in the document. You can scroll down in the Pages panel to see thumbnails of all eight pages.

2 In the Pages panel, double-click the Page 2 thumbnail

To move to the second page. This is a facing-pages document, so both pages 2 and 3 are visible, although the view is centered on page 2. The tooltip shows the name of the master page applied to this page.

3 In the status bar, observe the page box	The page box shows that you are viewing page 2 in the document.
On the right side of the page box, click the down-facing arrow	To display the list of pages in the document.
From the page list, select **4**	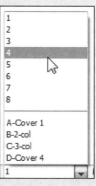
	To go to page 4.
4 From the page list, select **1**	To return to the first page.
5 Point anywhere on the page and hold (SPACEBAR)	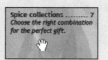
	To temporarily select the Hand tool. The pointer changes to a hand icon.
Drag up	As you drag, the document moves, and a different portion of the layout is visible.
Drag until you can see the top of the second spread	
6 Point to the bottom of the first page, hold (CTRL) + (SPACEBAR), and click twice	To zoom in on the bottom of the page.
7 Press (CTRL) + (0)	To zoom to Fit Page in Window. The selected page fits in the document window.
Press (CTRL) + (1)	To zoom to Actual Size.
Fit the page in the window	Press Ctrl+0.
8 Click the Arrange Documents button	(In the group of buttons to the right of the menu bar.) To display a menu.
Choose **New Window**	To open a new window for the current document.
Navigate to page 8	

9 Choose **File**, **Open...**	You'll open another document.
In the current topic folder, select **Outlander address**	
Click **Open**	To open the document in a new tab.
Navigate to page 2 and press ⌈CTRL⌉ + ⌈1⌉	
Click the tab for the **Outlander Sample.indd:2** window	To activate this window.
10 From the Arrange Documents menu, choose ▣	(3-Up.) To arrange the windows. This is a good way to view different parts of a document at the same time or to compare different documents.
11 Choose **File**, **Close**	To close the third window.
Close the second window	Choose File, Close.

The Tools, Control, and Info panels

Explanation   The tools and basic options for adding and modifying text and graphics are located in the Tools panel and the Control panel. The Info panel offers additional detail about objects in a document.

The Tools panel

The Tools panel is, by default, docked to the left of the application window. To see the name of a tool, point to it to display a tooltip. Some tools have a small black triangle in the bottom-right corner. If you hold down the mouse button on these tools, they expand to show similar tools. For example, if you expand the Rectangle Frame tool, you can also select the Ellipse Frame tool or the Polygon Frame tool. The following table describes the tools in the Tools panel.

Tool	Description
	Use the Selection tool to select, move, and resize frames.
	Use the Direct Selection tool to select the contents of a frame or to work with editable objects such as paths or frame corners.
	Use the Page tool to select a page and then change the page size. This tool lets you create multiple page sizes within a document.
	Use the Gap tool to adjust the size of a gap between two or more objects.
T — T Type Tool T \ — Type on a Path Tool Shift+T	Use the Type tool to enter and edit text. Use the Type on a Path tool to flow text along a path or shape.
	Use the Line tool to draw straight lines.
■ Pen Tool P Add Anchor Point Tool = Delete Anchor Point Tool - Convert Direction Point Tool Shift+C	Use the Pen, Add Anchor Point, Delete Anchor Point, and Convert Direction Point tools to draw and edit curved or straight lines and to adjust the shape of frames.
■ Pencil Tool N Smooth Tool Erase Tool	Use the Pencil, Smooth, and Erase tools to draw and edit freeform paths, as if you were drawing by hand on paper.
■ Rectangle Frame Tool F Ellipse Frame Tool Polygon Frame Tool	Use the Rectangle Frame, Ellipse Frame, and Polygon Frame tools to draw graphics frames of different shapes.

Tool	Description
Rectangle Tool M / Ellipse Tool L / Polygon Tool	Use the Rectangle, Ellipse, and Polygon tools to draw shapes.
✂	Use the Scissors tool to cut lines or text paths into two or more parts.
Free Transform Tool E / Rotate Tool R / Scale Tool S / Shear Tool O	Use the Free Transform tool to rotate, scale, and shear graphics or text. Use the Rotate tool to rotate items. Use the Scale tool to scale graphics or text. Use the Shear tool to shear graphics or text.
▨	Use the Gradient Swatch tool to apply or edit gradient fills.
▨	Use the Gradient Feather tool to fade the applied gradient fill to transparent.
📝	Use the Note tool to add nonprinting editorial notes to a document.
Eyedropper Tool I / Measure Tool K	Use the Eyedropper tool to sample color settings from an object in an InDesign document, including imported graphics. Use the Measure tool to calculate the distance between two points in the document window.
✋	Use the Hand tool to scroll through the document.
🔍	Use the Zoom tool to zoom in and out.

At the bottom of the Tools panel are buttons for applying color formatting to an object's stroke and fill. There is also a button for changing the document view—hold the mouse button and select Normal, Preview, Bleed, or Slug view.

The Control panel

You can view properties for selected items and apply formatting by using the Control panel. When you select the Type tool, the Control panel displays character and paragraph formatting properties. When you select a graphic, shape, or frame, the Control panel displays the properties of that item, as shown in Exhibit 1-6. To change properties for a selected item, type values in the appropriate boxes and then press Enter. For some properties, you can also adjust values incrementally by clicking the small arrows next to the text boxes.

The Reference Point indicator is located on the left side of the Control panel. When you're adjusting the size or position of objects, clicking a reference point tells InDesign to size or position the object relative to a fixed point on the object.

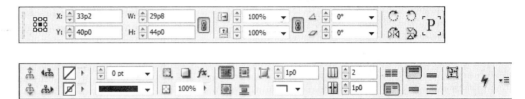

Exhibit 1-6: The Control panel displaying the properties of a selected item

The following table describes some of the properties and actions available in the Control panel when a graphic, shape, or frame is selected.

Property	Description
X	The horizontal position (X-coordinate) of a graphic, shape, or frame on a page.
Y	The vertical position (Y-coordinate) of a graphic, shape, or frame on a page.
W	The width of a graphic, shape, or frame.
H	The height of a graphic, shape, or frame.
100%	Scales a graphic, shape, or frame horizontally.
100%	Scales a graphic, shape, or frame vertically.
0°	The angle of rotation for a graphic, shape, or frame.
0°	The angle of shear for a graphic, shape, or frame.
C	Rotates a graphic, shape, or frame clockwise by 90 degrees.
	Rotates a graphic, shape, or frame counterclockwise by 90 degrees.
	Flips a graphic, shape, or frame horizontally.
	Flips a graphic, shape, or frame vertically.
P	Shows the flipped state of a graphic, shape, or frame.

Property	Description
	Selects the container, content, previous object, or next object.
0 pt	Sets the weight and style of a border around a graphic, shape, or frame.
fx. 100%	Sets the effects, transparency, and opacity of a graphic, shape, or frame.
	Sets the text wrap options for a graphic, shape, or frame.

The Info panel

As with the Control panel, the information displayed in the Info panel depends on what you have selected in a document. When you select an object with either the Selection or Direct Selection tool, for example, the Info panel displays information about the object. This information includes the object's width and height, and if you move the object, shows the distance and angle at which you have moved it. In addition, the Info panel displays the X and Y coordinates of the pointer. (The Control panel, in contrast, displays the X and Y coordinates of a selected object's reference point. If no object is selected, however, the Control panel displays the X and Y coordinates of the pointer.)

If you place the insertion point in a story, the Info panel tells you the number of characters, words, lines, and paragraphs in the story. The Info panel also provides information on colors applied to an object and about graphics placed in the document.

Do it! **A-3: Examining basic panels**

Here's how	Here's why
1 Go to page 5	In the Pages panel, double-click the Page 5 thumbnail.
2 In the Tools panel, point to the indicated tool	The name of the tool appears as a tooltip. The tooltip also indicates the shortcut keys you can press to select the tool.
3 Click T.	To select the Type tool.
Observe the Control panel	Because no text is selected, it displays the default character formatting properties.
Click within the heading **Spicy Buzzard Wings**	(At the top of page 5.) The Control panel now displays the formatting of the selected text.
4 Choose **Window, Info**	To open the Info panel. It displays the location of the insertion point on the page; the dimensions of the text frame; and the number of characters, words, lines, and paragraphs in the story.
5 In the Tools panel, click and hold	(The Pen tool.) To display the additional tools for drawing curved segments: Add Anchor Point, Delete Anchor Point, and Convert Direction Point.

6 Click

The Selection tool.

Click the plate-of-food graphic

At the bottom of page 5.

Observe the Control panel

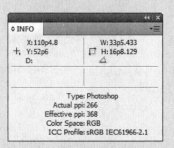

The X and Y location boxes display the coordinates of the top-left corner of the graphics frame. (Note the Reference Point indicator.) The W and H boxes display the width and height of the graphics frame.

Observe the Info panel

‡ INFO

X:110p4.8   W:33p5.433
+, Y:52p6   ⊏⁺ H:16p8.129
D: △

Type: Photoshop
Actual ppi: 266
Effective ppi: 368
Color Space: RGB
ICC Profile: sRGB IEC61966-2.1

The X and Y values indicate the pointer's position in the layout. The W and H values display the width and height of the selected graphics frame. In addition, there is information about the graphic.

7 Click the Info panel tab, as shown

W:33p5.433
H:16p8.129
△

(At the top-right of the Info panel.) To close the Info panel.

8 Choose **File**, **Close**

To close the document.

If prompted to save the document, click **No**

Topic B: Preferences and defaults

Explanation

You can customize InDesign to suit your working preferences. For example, you can change the color of guides or modify the appearance of the Tools panel. You change preferences by choosing an option from the Edit, Preferences submenu to open the Preferences dialog box, shown in Exhibit 1-7. The left column in the dialog box contains category options.

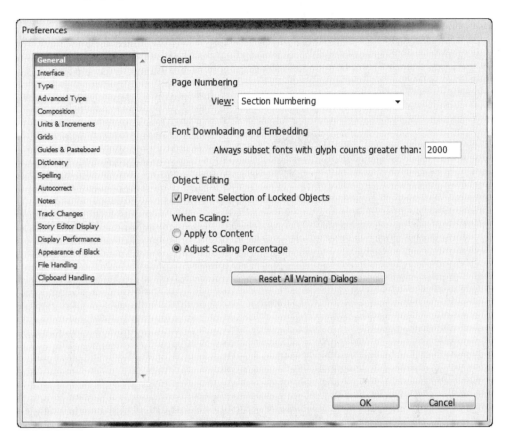

Exhibit 1-7: The Preferences dialog box

Application and document preferences

When no document is open, changes made in preference settings will apply to all documents. These preferences will then apply to any document you open. Preferences that apply to the application, rather than to a specific document, include the following: General, Interface, Spelling, Autocorrect, Notes, Story Editor Display, Display Performance, Appearance of Black, and Clipboard Handling.

When a document is open, however, some changes in preferences apply to only that document. For example, if you change the color of ruler guides with a document open, other existing documents and any new documents will continue to use the default color. Preferences that apply to any open document (when a document is open) include the following: Composition, Units & Increments, and Grids.

Other preference categories include a mix of settings that can apply either to the application or to an open document.

To change preferences, choose Edit, Preferences and then choose a category, such as General or Type. (Once the Preferences dialog box is open, you can select any of the categories to set those preferences.) Each category has its own options that appear on the right side of the dialog box. The following table describes some commonly used preferences.

Category	Option	Description
General	When Scaling	By default, InDesign displays an object's scale percentage in the Control panel as 100%, even after you've scaled it. Select Adjust Scaling Percentage to show the percentage an object has been scaled relative to its original size in the layout.
Type	Drag and Drop Text Editing	Check Enable in Layout View to cut, copy, and paste text in a story by dragging with the mouse rather than by using menu or keyboard commands.
Composition	Highlight	Select options to highlight elements of the document you might want to change, such as widows and orphans.
Units & Increments	Ruler Units	Change the horizontal and vertical ruler units, and set the origin (that is, 0, 0) of the rulers.
Autocorrect	Enable Autocorrect	Check this option to automatically correct commonly misspelled words as you type them.
Display Performance	Options	Specify the default view of graphics placed in a document. The default setting is Typical. The Fast setting draws graphics as gray shapes, which is useful for scrolling through graphics-heavy documents. The High Quality setting is good for adjusting detail but might affect performance.
Display Performance	Adjust View Settings	Select individual quality settings for raster images, vector graphics, and transparencies. Anti-aliasing makes type and bitmap images easier to see by smoothing the edges. The Greek Type Below setting makes type at a specific size appear as a gray bar, increasing performance.

Global and document defaults

As with Preferences, changes made in any settings while a document is open apply to that document only. On the other hand, changes made in document settings when no document is open are global—they apply to all new documents but don't affect existing documents. For example, if you create a new swatch while a document is open, it is available in that document only. If you create a new swatch when no document is open, it is available in all new documents, but not in any existing documents.

Do it!

B-1:   Setting preferences

The files for this activity are in Student Data folder **Unit 1\Topic B**.

Here's how	Here's why
1 Display the Open dialog box	
Navigate to the current topic folder and double-click **Outlander Sample**	To open the document.
Click **Update Links**	
2 Choose **Edit**, **Preferences**, **General...**	To open the Preferences dialog box with the General options displayed.
3 Under When Scaling, select **Adjust Scaling Percentage**	This setting keeps the scale value set to the percentage you scale an object. The default, Apply to Content, resets an object's scale value in the Control panel to 100% after you've scaled it.
4 In the category list, select **Type**	To display the Type preferences.
5 Under Drag and Drop Text Editing, check **Enable in Layout View**	With this option, you can drag and drop text in the layout, similar to the way you'd do that in a word processor.
6 In the category list, select **Units & Increments**	The default unit of measurement is picas. This unit is commonly used in publishing, but you can specify a different unit of measure.
7 In the category list, select **Display Performance**	If you have a slow computer or are working with documents that have many objects, especially large photos, you can change these settings for better performance.
8 Click **OK**	To close the dialog box.
9 Choose **File**, **Close**	To close the document.
If prompted to save the document, click **No**	

Topic C: InDesign Help

Explanation

When you are working with InDesign, you might need help with its features and tools. You can find information by using the Adobe Community Help Web site. To do so, press F1 or choose Help, InDesign Help.

Adobe Community Help

When you choose InDesign Help from the Help menu, the Adobe Community Help site opens in Adobe AIR. The window is divided into two panes, as shown in Exhibit 1-8. The right pane contains a toolbar with a link on it. Click that link to get access to the complete Adobe Community Help content in a Web browser.

Adobe Community Help contains the latest in online product documentation, articles, tutorials, videos, and moderated questions and answers in the Adobe AIR environment. (AIR, or Adobe Integrated Runtime, is a cross-platform runtime environment designed for developing Internet-based applications.) When AIR is not connected to the Internet, a local version of Help is available.

Searching Help

Once Adobe Community Help is open, you can access content in either pane. In the left pane, use the Search box to find help on a particular item. Type the desired text in the Search box and press Enter. The system searches not only the titles of help topics, but also their contents. The results are displayed in the left pane and include all topics that include at least one occurrence of the word you typed. Click the desired result in the left pane, and the corresponding content will appear in the right pane for you to read.

Help Topics

When Adobe Community Help is first opened, you'll find a list of help topics in the right pane. Click the plus sign to the left of a topic to expand it. Click each topic title to display help for that topic. Use the buttons on the toolbar to return to the Home page, go back, go forward, and refresh the content.

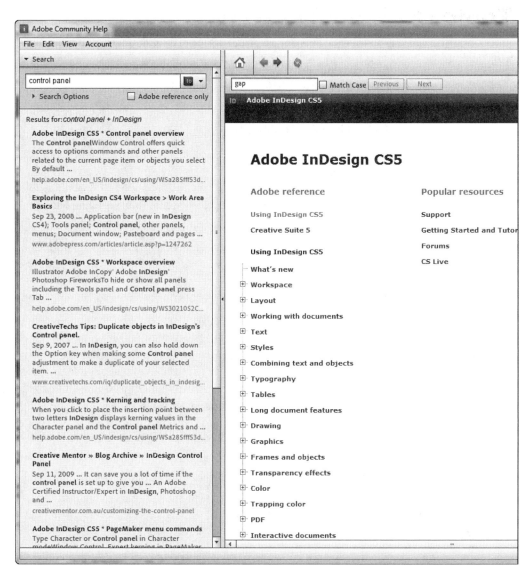

Exhibit 1-8: Searching help topics in Adobe Community Help

Do it!

C-1: Using Help

Here's how	Here's why
1 Choose **Help**, **InDesign Help...**	To open Adobe Community Help in the Adobe AIR environment.
2 In the Search box, enter **control panel** Press `← ENTER`	 Near the top-left corner of the window.
3 Observe the list of search results	

The results preceded by "Adobe InDesign CS5 *" are links to help topics. Other links might take you to other content areas.

4 Click **Adobe InDesign CS5 * Control panel overview**	To view information about the Control panel in InDesign Help.
In the right pane, read the article	Scroll down to see all the content.
5 Close Adobe Community Help	To return to InDesign.

Unit summary: Getting started

Topic A   In this topic, you explored the **InDesign environment** and learned how to navigate a document by scrolling and zooming. You also learned about **panels** and **workspaces**.

Topic B   In this topic, you learned how to set **preferences**, global and document defaults, and **object attributes**.

Topic C   In this topic, you learned how to access **Adobe Community Help**.

Independent practice activity

In this activity, you'll open an InDesign document, navigate among pages, and use InDesign Help.

The files for this activity are in Student Data folder **Unit 1\Unit summary**.

1 Open Outlander sample. Update the links if necessary.

2 Navigate to each page in the document.

3 Navigate to page 5.

4 Change the magnification to 200%.

5 View the spice images at the top of the page.

6 Click one of the images to select it, and observe the selected graphic frame's width and height values.

7 Close the document without saving changes.

8 Open Adobe Community Help.

9 Search for help on **panels**.

10 Click an item in the list of results to display its corresponding information.

11 Close Adobe Community Help.

Review questions

1 How can you display a panel to see its contents?

  A In the collapsed panel dock, click the panel's name.

  B From the Window menu, choose the desired panel's name.

  C At the top of the panel dock, click the Expand Panels icon, and then click the desired panel's tab.

  D All of the above.

2 Which panels display the W and H values of a selected object? [Choose all that apply.]

  A The Object Styles panel

  B The Control panel

  C The Info panel

  D The Pages panel

3 Which keys can you press to temporarily access the Zoom tool?

  A Ctrl+Shift

  B Ctrl+Alt

  C Ctrl+Shift+Alt

  D Ctrl+Spacebar

4 Which panel displays the X and Y coordinates of a selected object? [Choose all that apply.]

  A The Control panel

  B The Info panel

  C The Pages panel

  D The Layers panel

5 You have one document open, and you open another document. It will appear in which of the following, by default?

  A A floating window in front of the current document window

  B A new panel

  C A floating window behind the current document window

  D A window tab

6 You want to find information about how to use InDesign's new options for viewing document windows. How can you do this from within InDesign?

  A Choose Help, InDesign Help, and then perform a search in Adobe Community Help.

  B Choose Window, Adobe Community Help to open the help system.

  C Choose Window, Info to open the Info panel.

  D You can't. You should use an Internet search engine.

Unit 2

Basic documents

Unit time: 60 minutes

Complete this unit, and you'll know how to:

A Create a document preset and create a document.

B Create text in InDesign and place a text file.

C Place graphics, and place pages from other InDesign documents.

D Create, apply, load, and save color swatches.

Topic A: New documents

This topic covers the following ACE exam objectives for InDesign CS5.

#	Objective
1.1	Create a new document with settings appropriate for print or onscreen display.
1.2	Adjust the size and position of one or more pages in a document with the Page tool.

Creating documents

Explanation

In InDesign, you can create single-page publications, such as flyers advertising a sale, or multi-page publications, such as newsletters advertising your company's newly released products. By default, a new InDesign document contains a single-page layout. You can create a multi-page layout by adding pages to the document.

To create a print document:

1 Choose File, New, Document to open the New Document dialog box (shown in Exhibit 2-1).

2 From the Intent list, select Print.

3 Specify the number of pages and whether the document will contain facing pages.

4 Select an option from the Page Size list, or enter a custom size in the Width and Height boxes. Select either a Portrait or Landscape orientation.

5 If necessary, set the number of columns, the width of the gutter between columns, and the margin settings.

6 Click OK.

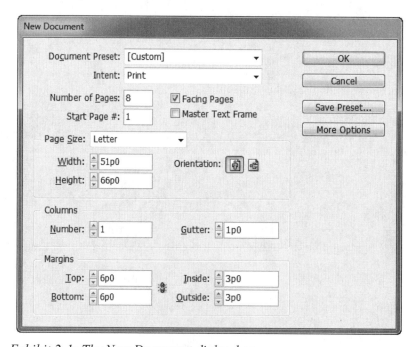

Exhibit 2-1: The New Document dialog box

To create a document for the Web, open the New Document dialog box. From the Intent list, select Web. Set the other desired options and click OK.

The following table describes components of the New Document dialog box.

Item	Description
Facing Pages	Select this option if your publication contains left- and right-facing pages—or *spreads*—as in a book, newspaper, or magazine spread. When you select this option, you can specify the inside margin—along the publication's spine—and the outside margin—along the outside edges of the left and right pages.
Master Text Frame	Check this box if you want InDesign to automatically insert a text frame the size of the area defined by the page margins.
Page Size	Specify the page size, which will depend on the type of publication you are creating. For example, a flyer or newsletter is likely to be Letter, while a newspaper is likely to be Tabloid. The Page Size list lets you choose from standard page sizes, such as Letter, Legal, Tabloid, US Business Card, or Compact Disc. You can also select one of the Web sizes, which range from 600×300 to 1280×800. To create pages with a custom size, enter the desired height and width in the Height and Width boxes.
Columns	You can have multiple columns of text on a single page, as in a newspaper or magazine. Use the Number box under Columns to specify the number of columns on each page. Specify the *gutter* width, or spacing between columns, in the Gutter box. By default, each page has one column.
Margins	To specify page margins, enter values in the Top, Bottom, Inside, and Outside boxes. If you clear Facing Pages, then Inside and Outside become Left and Right.

Document presets

You might need to create several documents that have similar dimensions or layout guides. Or you might find that you are creating different kinds of documents—such as flyers, newsletters, and magazine ads—that have similar dimensions or layout properties customized for your particular needs. Rather than specifying settings in the New Document dialog box each time you create a document, you can save *document presets* that include these custom settings.

To create a document preset, follow these steps:

1   Choose File, Document Presets, Define to open the Document Presets dialog box.

2   Click New.

3   In the New Document Preset dialog box, select the settings you want to use for the preset, as you would when creating a document.

4   Click More Options if you want to specify Bleed and Slug settings. A *bleed* is any item that extends off the edge of the page to ensure that no white gaps appear between the item and the edge of the paper. The *slug* is the area that contains printing and customized color bar information or instructions regarding other aspects of the document.

5   In the Document Preset box, enter a name for the preset.

6   Click OK.

After you have created a document preset, you can use it to create a document by choosing File, Document Presets and choosing the preset from the submenu. You can also select a preset from the Document Preset list in the New Document dialog box.

Measurement systems

InDesign uses picas as the default unit of measure. The traditional measurement system used for typesetting is picas and points, and many designers and typesetters still use this measurement system. Moreover, font size is measured in points, so it's generally more convenient if all units of measure in the document match.

To change the unit of measure, choose Edit, Preferences, Units & Increments to open the Preferences dialog box with the Units & Increments settings active. Select a unit of measure from the Horizontal and Vertical lists, and click OK.

If you're new to the picas and points measurement system, the following conversions may be helpful:

- 72 points = 1 inch
- 12 points = 1 pica
- 6 picas = 1 inch

The following table describes the notation used in InDesign to denote values using the picas and points measurement system.

Example	Value	Description
3p7	3 picas, 7 points	The value before the "p" represents picas, and the value after the "p" represents points. (There are 12 points in 1 pica, so for example, 3p12 is equivalent to 4p0.)
0p3 or 3 pt	3 points	You can designate a value in points by entering a value after the letter "p" or before "pt."

Inserting pages

You can insert pages in a document as necessary. One way to do this is to choose Layout, Pages, Add Page. No dialog box opens, but a single page is added after the current page. To insert more than one page at a time, use the Insert Pages dialog box, shown in Exhibit 2-2:

1 Open the Insert Pages dialog box.

- Choose Layout, Pages, Insert Pages.
- Activate the Pages panel and choose Insert Pages from the panel menu.

2 In the Pages box, enter the number of pages you want to insert.

3 From the Insert list, select After Page, Before Page, At Start of Document, or At End of Document. If you select After Page or Before Page, specify the page after or before which you want to insert the new pages.

4 Specify which master page (if any) to apply to the new pages. *Master pages* act as templates within a document.

If you just want to add multiple pages to the end of the document, you can also choose File, Document Setup and enter a value in the Number of Pages box. InDesign will add blank pages to the end of the document.

Exhibit 2-2: The Insert Pages dialog box

Inserting pages from within the Pages panel

You can also insert pages from within the Pages panel. To do this, drag the page icon or master-page icon to a location among the existing page or spread icons, as shown in Exhibit 2-3. If the document contains facing pages, this method will create new spreads.

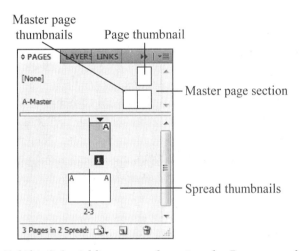

Exhibit 2-3: Adding pages by using the Pages panel

The Page tool

InDesign's new Page tool enables you to create multiple page sizes in the same document. The Page tool is easy to use: select the tool, point to a page, and click. When you select a page, the Control panel displays the Page tool controls, as shown in Exhibit 2-4.

Exhibit 2-4: The Page tool controls in the Control panel

You can use the Width and Height boxes to create a custom page size or use the drop-down list to select a standard page size, such as Letter, Legal, Tabloid, or A4. To the right of the drop-down list are two buttons, Portrait and Landscape, that you can use to change the page orientation.

On the right side of the Control panel, there are three check boxes:

- **Enable Layout Adjustment** — Check this box before you change the page size, margins, or columns. Then when you make those changes, the layout elements (text and graphics frames) are automatically adjusted to fit the new layout.

- **Show Master Page Overlay** — Check this box to display a shaded box over the selected page. Once the master page overlay is displayed, you can move it to another location on the page.

- **Objects Move with Page** — Check this box to make objects on the page move when you change the selected page's X and Y values.

Saving a document

To save a document, choose File, Save As to open the Save As dialog box. Navigate to the location where you want to save the file, enter a file name for the document, and click Save. To update a document you've already saved, choose File, Save.

Do it!

A-1: Creating a new document

Here's how	Here's why
1 Choose **File**, **New**, **Document...**	To open the New Document dialog box. You will create an eight-page document.
2 Edit the Number of Pages box to read **8**	
3 Under Columns, edit the Number box to read **2**	To create column guides in the document.
4 Observe the Margins section	Margins Top: 3p0 Inside: 3p0 Bottom: 3p0 Outside: 3p0
	(At the bottom of the dialog box.) By default, the margins are set to 3p0 (which is the same as 0.5") for all sides. You want the top and bottom margins to be set to 6p0 (1").
Click the button	The button changes to an unlink icon so you can change an individual margin without changing all of the margins.
Under Margins, edit the Top box to read **6**	Margins Top: 6 Bottom: 3p0
Press (TAB)	To move to the next box—in this case, the Bottom box—and select its contents.
Type **6** and press (TAB)	Margins Top: 6p0 Bottom: 6p0
5 Click **Save Preset**	To open the Save Preset dialog box.
Edit the Save Preset As box to read **My preset**	
Click **OK**	To close the dialog box. The preset now appears in the Document Preset list.
6 Click **OK**	To close the dialog box and create the document.
7 Expand the Pages panel	(If necessary.) In the docked panels on the right side of the window, click Pages.
Observe the panel's contents	The document contains eight pages in five spreads. The first and last pages are each single-page spreads, and the first page is selected.

8	Select	To select the Page tool.
	Observe the mouse pointer	 It has changed shape to include a page icon.
9	Point to the page and click	To select page 1.
10	Observe the Control panel	It contains the controls associated with the Page tool.
	Click	(The Landscape button in the Control panel.) To change the page orientation from Portrait to Landscape.
	Display the page-size list and select **Letter – Half**	 To change the page size for the selected page. The other pages in the document are still Letter size with a Landscape orientation.
11	Observe the Pages panel	Page 1 is resized and has a Landscape page orientation.
12	Click	(The Portrait button in the Control panel.) To return the page orientation to Portrait.
	Display the page-size list and select **Letter**	To change the page size.
13	Click	The Selection tool.
	Click in the pasteboard	To deselect the page.
14	Choose **File**, **Save As**	To open the Save As dialog box.
	Navigate to the current topic folder	
	Edit the File Name box to read **My newsletter**	
	Click **Save**	To save the document.

Topic B: Text frames

This topic covers the following ACE exam objective for InDesign CS5.

#	Objective
2.5	Manipulate text flow by using text threading, smart text reflow, resizing, and text wrap.

Using text frames

Explanation

In InDesign, you place and arrange text in a document by using text frames. To work with text, you can create a space for it by creating a text frame with the Type tool. You can also place text documents created in another application and have InDesign create the text frame automatically.

Text frames let you place text exactly where you want it on a page, so you might want to use separate text frames for different text elements. For example, if you have more than one article on a page (as in a magazine or newspaper), you can place each article in its own text frame. This will allow you to position each article where you want it and to size each text frame independently.

With the Type tool selected, drag the pointer anywhere in your document to create a text frame. After you've created a text frame, you can use the Selection tool to adjust its size and position to fit the layout.

To add text to a text frame, you can type the text, copy and paste text into the text frame (for example, from another InDesign document or another application), or place text from an external file. A red plus sign appears at the bottom of a text frame if the frame is too small to display all the text it contains. You can resize the text frame by using the Selection tool to drag its corner and side handles; you can also double-click the side, top, or bottom handles of a text frame to resize it automatically to fit the contents of the frame.

If you want to edit the contents of a text frame, either use the Type tool to place the insertion point or double-click a text frame with the Selection tool.

Selecting text

There are several ways to select text for editing or formatting. Using the Type tool, you can:

- Click twice on a word to select that word.
- Click three times anywhere on a line to select that line of text.
- Click four times anywhere in a paragraph to select that paragraph.
- Click five times anywhere in a text frame to select all text in a *story* (text contained in a series of threaded frames).

Any text formatting you choose will be applied to the selected text.

Applying character formatting

You have many options for formatting text. You can view and modify character formatting, as shown in Exhibit 2-5, by clicking the Character Formatting Controls button in the left section of the Control panel. The Control panel menu contains additional character formatting options. In addition, you can use the Swatches and Color panels to apply color to selected text.

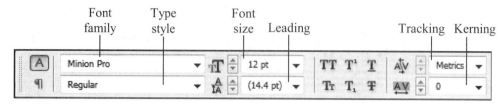

Exhibit 2-5: Character formatting options in the Control panel

The following table lists some character formatting attributes you can change.

Item	Description
Font family	Choose from fonts installed on your computer.
Type style	Use type styles such as italic to add emphasis to the text. Bold might be useful for headlines or subheadings.
Font size	Typically, 10- or 12-point type is easy to read and is used for body text. Headlines might be any size, but 24- to 60-point type will get a reader's attention. You can use different type sizes to draw attention to specific document elements.
Leading	Measured in points, this is the vertical space allocated to each line of text in a paragraph. (This is not the same as spacing between paragraphs.) The default is auto. For 12-point type, auto is equivalent to 14.4-point leading, or 1.2 times the font size.
Kerning	Kerning is the horizontal space between a specific set of characters. The default is 0. Kerning is measured relative to particular fonts, which means that changing fonts will change the kerning proportionally.
Tracking	Use tracking to tighten or loosen a block of text. Adjusting tracking will not affect any kerning you have applied.

When you display the Font Family list, you see a preview of the selected typeface. To the right of the font name, the text "Sample" has the font family applied to it so that you can see what the font will look like before applying it to your text.

Specifying leading

Leading is the measurement of space between the baseline of one line of text and the baseline of the next line. The *baseline* is the horizontal position on which a line of type sits. Some lowercase letters—g, j, p, q, and y—descend below the baseline.

By default, InDesign uses auto leading, which creates a leading value of 120% of the largest type size on a line. Therefore, if the largest type size on a line is 10 points, the leading would be 12 points (120% of 10 points).

Auto leading can sometimes produce unintended results. For example, if you have more than one type size in a block of text, different lines will have different leading values.

To avoid this problem, you can set a fixed leading amount. Moreover, specifying higher leading values often makes text easier to read and adds visual interest. Observe Exhibit 2-6, which shows body text using the default auto leading, compared to the same text with a higher fixed leading value.

Exhibit 2-6: A paragraph using the Auto leading setting (left), and set to fixed 18-point leading (right)

To set a fixed leading amount:

1 Select the text.
2 In the Control panel, in the Leading box, type the leading value (in points).
3 Press Enter.

You can change the leading value in single increments by clicking the up arrow or down arrow to the left of the Leading box, or you can select a value from the drop-down list.

Do it!

B-1: Creating text in a document

The files for this activity are in Student Data folder **Unit 2\Topic B**.

Here's how	Here's why
1 Open Newsletter2	From the current topic folder.
Choose **File**, **Save As**	You'll save this document with a different name.
Edit the File name box to read **My Newsletter2**	
Click **Save**	To save the publication in the current topic folder.
2 Go to page 5	In the Pages panel, double-click the Page 5 thumbnail.
3 Choose **View**, **Extras**	To display the Extras submenu.
Observe the options	

Hide Frame Edges	Ctrl+H
Show Text Threads	Alt+Ctrl+Y
Show Assigned Frames	
Hide Hyperlinks	
Hide Notes	
Hide Content Grabber	
Hide Live Corners	

If "Hide Frame Edges" appears in the menu, then objects' frame edges are set to be visible, giving you visual clues about the placement of objects. If frame edges are hidden, the Extras submenu displays "Show Frame Edges" instead.

You'll create frames and add content to them.

4 Select the Type tool	(In the Tools panel.) You'll create a large heading near the top of the page.

5 Point near the top and left margin guides, and then drag down and to the right as shown

To create a text frame. Using the smart cursor information to guide you, draw a text box that is about 10p wide and 5p high. Next, you'll add some text.

Observe the text frame

The text frame displays a blinking insertion point.

6 Press CTRL + 2

To view the document at 200% magnification. Because InDesign zooms centered on the insertion point, you might need to scroll the document to see the whole text frame.

7 Type **Spicy Buzzard Wings**

You'll make the headline bigger and apply a different font.

8 Choose **Edit**, **Select All**

To select all the text you typed.

Observe the Character Formatting Controls in the Control panel

The default font family is Minion Pro.

9 From the Font Family list, select **Trebuchet MS**

From the Type Style list, select **Bold**

From the Font Size list, select **36 pt**

10 Observe the text frame

The text might no longer fit in the text frame. If that's the case, the small red plus sign in the bottom-right corner of a text frame indicates that there is more text than is visible in the frame. To see the overset text, you'll make the text frame larger.

11 Using the Selection tool, drag the text frame to snap it to the top and left margin guides

If necessary.

12 Point to the middle-right handle of the text frame, as shown

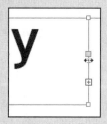

The pointer changes to a double-sided arrow.

Drag to align the frame with the right page margin

13 Double-click the bottom handle of the text frame

To automatically change the frame's height to fit the contents.

14 Choose **File**, **Save**

To update the document.

Placing text

Explanation   Although you can enter text directly into documents, you will also probably place text that has been written and edited in another application, such as Microsoft Word. You can place text into an existing text frame, but if you place text without adding it to a text frame, InDesign will automatically create a text frame.

To place text in an existing text frame:

1   Click the Type tool.
2   Click inside a text frame to place the insertion point.
3   Choose File, Place and navigate to the file you want to place. Select the file.
4   Click Open.

To place text independently of any existing text frames, first make sure nothing on the page is selected. Then choose File, Place and select the file you want to place. When you click Open, the pointer will turn into a loaded-text icon. Click or drag to create a new text frame containing the text.

Do it!

B-2: Placing text

The files for this activity are in Student Data folder **Unit 2\Topic B**.

Here's how	Here's why
1 Press ⌨CTRL + ⌨0	To view the entire page.
2 Click the Type tool	You'll import some text from a Microsoft Word document.
Drag from the left margin guide to the first column guide, as shown	**Spicy Buzzard Wings**
	Below the headline, draw a text box that is 22p wide by 16p high.
3 Choose **File**, **Place...**	To open the Place dialog box.
Navigate to the current topic folder	If necessary.
Select **Ingredients.docx** and click **Open**	To place the Microsoft Word document.
Using the Selection tool, double-click the bottom handle of the text frame	To resize the frame to fit the text.
4 Choose **Edit**, **Deselect All**	To deselect all page elements. You will place more text, but not in a text frame you have already created.
5 Choose **File**, **Place...**	
In the current topic folder, double-click **Directions.docx**	To load the text file into the pointer.

6	Observe the pointer	It indicates that text is loaded and available to place.
	Click in the column to the right of the ingredients text	To place the text in a new text frame. The text frame automatically fills the width of the column.
	Resize the bottom of the text frame to fit the text	Double-click the bottom handle of the text frame.
7	Update and close the document	(Choose File, Save.) To save the changes.

Topic C: Graphics frames

This topic covers the following ACE exam objectives for InDesign CS5.

#	Objective
4.1	Given a scenario, determine the best settings for choosing and placing an image.
4.4	Hide or show layers in placed PSD, AI, INDD, and PDF files, and discuss how image transparency is handled.

Graphics

Explanation

Graphics can enhance the look of a document and convey information. Varying the sizes of your graphics can help readers discern which items in a document are most important and can enhance the flow and readability of your document.

Placing graphics is similar to placing text. You can place a graphic in a frame you have already drawn, or you can have InDesign automatically create a frame when you place the graphic. To place a graphic in an existing frame:

1 Using the Selection tool, click the frame in which you want to place the graphic.

2 Choose File, Place and navigate to the file you want to import. Select the file. (By default, Replace Selected Item is selected.)

3 Click Open. The graphic appears in the frame (unless the option to Replace Selected Item in the Place dialog box was cleared).

4 If the graphic is larger than the frame, you can resize the frame. You can also reposition the graphic within the frame.

5 If necessary, use the Selection tool to drag the frame to the desired location on the page. If you press Shift as you drag, the graphics frame moves only vertically or only horizontally (depending on how you drag).

To place a graphic independently of any existing page elements, first make sure nothing on the page is selected. Choose File, Place, and double-click the graphic file to load it into the pointer. Click a blank area of your layout to place the full-size image, or drag to create a frame at the desired size—the graphic will fill the frame at the size you draw it. Alternatively, you can place a graphic file that's loaded into the pointer by clicking an empty frame in the layout.

Moving a graphic within a frame

Once you have placed a graphic, you might need to reposition the image within the frame. The easiest way to do this is to use the new *content grabber* feature, as shown in Exhibit 2-7.

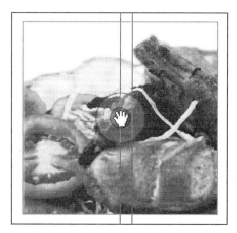

Exhibit 2-7: The new content grabber feature

To use the content grabber on a graphic within a frame:

1 Using the Selection tool, point to the graphics frame. (You don't have to select the frame.) The content grabber circle appears in the middle of the frame.

2 Point to the circle; the mouse pointer changes to the Hand tool.

3 Drag to reposition the image within the frame. When you release the mouse button, the Selection tool is selected.

To hide the content grabber, choose View, Extras, Hide Content Grabber.

You can also reposition a graphic within a frame by using the Direct Selection tool or by choosing any of the following commands from the Object, Fitting menu:

- Fill Frame Proportionally
- Fit Content Proportionally
- Fit Frame to Content
- Fit Content to Frame
- Center Content

Placing multiple files

You can place several files in one step. To do so, open the Place dialog box, and select any combination of text and graphic files by pressing Ctrl and clicking each file you want to place. To select a continuous range of files, click the first file, and then press Shift and click the last file in the range you want to select. After you click Open, a thumbnail image of the first file you selected appears in the pointer, along with the number of files you've selected. You can use the arrow keys to cycle through the loaded files before you click to place them. You can then click to place each file one at a time, or you can press Esc to "unload" the loaded files.

Changing the stacking order

As you add graphics and text, the frames might overlap each other. By default, each new frame you create is positioned at the top of the stacking order. This means that new items will overlap existing ones. However, you might want an item that is in front of another item to appear behind it.

To change the stacking order, select an item, choose Object, Arrange, and choose the command you want: Bring to Front, Bring Forward, Send Backward, or Send to Back. The Bring Forward and Send Backward commands move items forward or backward one position in the stacking order. The Bring to Front and Send to Back commands move items to the front of or behind all other items.

Graphics formats

You can place many types of graphics. For documents intended for print, TIFF or PSD (Photoshop) images are likely to give you the best results and the most flexibility with photographs, while EPS images are usually best for vector illustrations. Graphics formats used on the Web, such as JPEG and GIF, generally aren't suitable for commercial printing.

Do it!

C-1: Placing graphics

The files for this activity are in Student Data folder **Unit 2\Topic C**.

Here's how	Here's why
1 Open Newsletter3	From the current topic folder.
Choose **File**, **Save As**	You'll rename the document.
Edit the File name box to read **My Newsletter3**	
Click **Save**	To save the document in the current topic folder.
2 In the Tools panel, click ⊠	(The Rectangle Frame tool.) This tool is grouped with two others—the Ellipse Frame and Polygon Frame tools. If you don't see the Rectangle Frame tool, click and hold whichever of these tools is available and then select the Rectangle Frame tool.
3 Drag to create a rectangle frame near the bottom of the page, as shown	

Create a frame that is 20p by 14p. The graphics frame contains a large "X," indicating that it's a graphics frame, rather than a text frame or a shape.

4   Choose **File**, **Place...**

To open the Place dialog box.

In the Common folder, navigate to the **Images** folder, select **Spicy buzzard wings**, and click **Open**

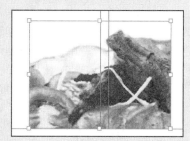

(The Common folder is in the Student Data folder.) The graphic appears in the graphics frame. Because the graphic is larger than the frame, only a portion of the graphic is visible.

5   In the Tools panel, click

The Selection tool.

6   Point to the graphic

The content grabber circle appears in the center of the frame.

Point to the content grabber

As you point, the mouse pointer changes to the Hand tool.

Drag to move the image within the frame, without releasing the mouse button

As you drag, you can see a preview of the entire graphic. The part that appears in the frame is clear, and the parts outside the frame are opaque.

Drag as shown

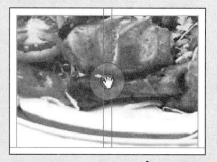

To align the bottom-left corner of the graphic with the bottom-left corner of the frame.

7 Using the Selection tool, select the graphics frame

   Choose **Object**, **Fitting**, **Fit Frame to Content**

To resize the frame so that it matches the size of the graphic.

8 Drag the graphic to the bottom-left corner of the layout

So that it snaps to the left and bottom margin guides.

9 Point to the top-right corner of the graphic

The pointer changes to a double-sided arrow. You'll resize the graphic.

   Hold CTRL + SHIFT and drag the top-right corner handle of the graphic

To resize the frame and the graphic together. Simply dragging the frame handles would resize only the frame while leaving the graphic unchanged. Holding Shift resizes the object proportionally.

   Drag to the left until the image is approximately 33 picas wide

10 Click a blank area of the page

To deselect all page elements. You will place some more graphics, but not in graphics frames you have already created.

11 Choose **File**, **Place...**

   Select **Cinnamon** and click **Open**

(In the Images folder, which is located in the Common folder.) The pointer changes to indicate that a graphic is loaded and available to place in the document. A thumbnail of the graphic appears with the pointer.

   Point to the pasteboard, to the right of the document page, and click

To place the graphic on the pasteboard.

12 Click a blank area of the pasteboard

To deselect all objects in the layout. If you don't deselect the graphic before placing the next one, then the one you place will replace the selected one.

13 Choose **File**, **Place...**	You'll place multiple files at the same time.
Select **Coriander**	(In the Images folder, located in the Common folder.) You'll also select Nutmeg. To select two items that aren't next to each other in the list, you'll press Ctrl as you select the second item.
Press ⌈CTRL⌋ and select **Nutmeg**	To select both Coriander and Nutmeg.
Click **Open**	The pointer changes to indicate that two graphics are available to place in the current document. You can press an arrow key to cycle through the icons for each graphic that's loaded.
14 Press an arrow key	To see the icon for the other graphic item that's loaded. You can use the arrow keys to cycle through the loaded graphics so you can place them in the order you want.
Click a blank area of the pasteboard	To place the first graphic.
15 Click below the graphic you just placed	To place the second graphic.
16 Update the document	

Placing InDesign pages

Explanation
In addition to placing text files and graphics, you can place entire InDesign pages into other InDesign documents. The new pages are placed as objects, rather than as editable InDesign pages.

To place an InDesign page:

1   Choose File, Place and navigate to the InDesign file you want to import. Select the file.

2   Check Show Import Options.

3   Click Open. The Place InDesign Document dialog box appears.

- On the General tab, select the pages you want to import and select a crop option.
- On the Layers tab, specify the layers you want to make visible.

4   Click OK.

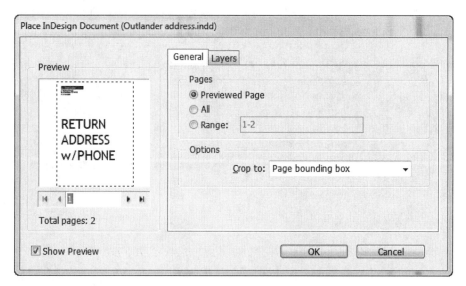

Exhibit 2-8: The General tab in the Place InDesign Document dialog box

You can't modify a placed page object directly, but you can change the original document, and the placed page object will automatically update to reflect the changes. This feature is particularly useful for things like letterhead, which might appear in many different documents but which you could update simply by editing the original linked document. You can open the original document by selecting the placed page object and choosing Edit, Edit Original.

If the InDesign file you've placed has layers, you can show or hide each layer after you've placed the file. To do so, select the placed file in the layout and choose Object, Object Layer Options. In the Object Layer Options dialog box, specify which layers you want to be visible or hidden.

Import options

When you place an image, graphic, or InDesign document, you can specify options such as which layers to show. The specific options available depend on what kind of object you're placing. For example, Exhibit 2-9 shows the options for placing a Photoshop image, while Exhibit 2-10 shows the options for placing an InDesign document.

For Photoshop images, you can select which layers to show in the placed image; similarly, for InDesign documents, you can select which pages to show and which layers should be visible. Likewise, when placing an Illustrator file, you can select which artboard to place.

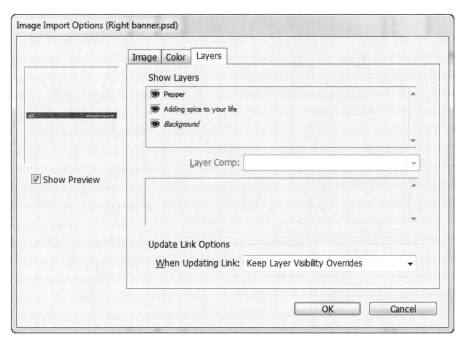

Exhibit 2-9: The Image Import Options dialog box

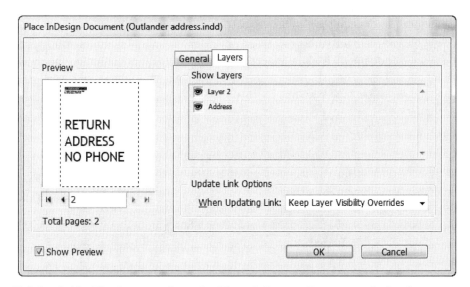

Exhibit 2-10: The Layers tab in the Place InDesign Document dialog box

Do it!

C-2: Placing InDesign pages

The files for this activity are in Student Data folder **Unit 2\Topic C**.

Here's how	Here's why
1 Go to page 8	You'll place a page from another InDesign document.
2 Choose **File**, **Place...**	
Navigate to the current topic folder and select **Outlander address**	
Check **Show Import Options**	
Click **Open**	To open the Place InDesign Document dialog box.
3 Under Preview, click the right arrow button	To go to page 2.
4 Under General, verify that **Previewed Page** is selected	To specify that you'll insert the page being previewed.
5 Click the **Layers** tab	
To the left of Layer 2, click the eye icon	Show Layers Layer 2 Address To hide the graphics layer.
Under Update Link Options, verify that **Keep Layer Visibility Overrides** is selected	So that the layer will stay hidden in this document if the link is updated.
6 Click **OK**	To load the page into the pointer and close the warning dialog box.
7 Click anywhere on page 8	To place the page as a graphic.
8 Drag the frame handles to crop the graphic as shown	**Outlander** Spices 1150 Grant Street San Francisco, CA 94113

9	Choose **Edit**, **Edit Original**	To open the document containing the original page. In a new document tab, InDesign opens the document to the page you placed. You will change the original document.
	Update the links	If necessary.
10	In the Outlander address document, go to page 2	If necessary.
	Edit the address as shown	
		Add a comma and "Suite 100" to the street address.
	Update and close Outlander address	
11	Click the document tab for **My newsletter3**	To see that InDesign has automatically updated the document based on the original.
	Observe the address	
12	Update and close My newsletter3	

Topic D: Custom colors

This topic covers the following ACE exam objective for InDesign CS5.

#	Objective
5.1	Explain the use of named swatches versus unnamed colors.

Using the New Color Swatch dialog box

Explanation

If your organization uses specific colors for a logo or other design elements, you can specify, apply, and store those colors in your InDesign documents. You can use a set of custom colors in your organization's print and online publications to maintain your organization's corporate identity, or brand.

You use the New Color Swatch dialog box, shown in Exhibit 2-11, to create a custom color.

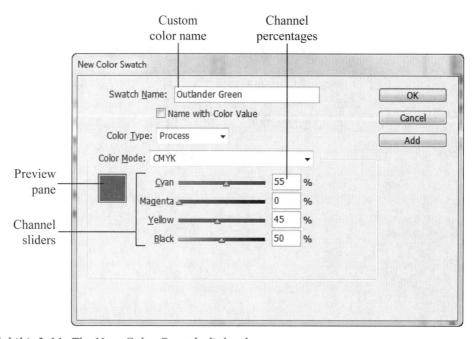

Exhibit 2-11: The New Color Swatch dialog box

To create a custom color:

1 In the Swatches panel, from the panel menu, choose New Color Swatch. (The panel menu button is in the top-right corner of the panel.)

2 Clear the Name with Color Value box (optional).

3 In the Swatch Name box, enter a name for the new color.

4 From the Color Type list, select Process or Spot.

5 From the Color Mode list, select a color mode. For print, use CMYK. For online publishing, use RGB.

6 Enter percentages for the color channels to create the color.

7 Click OK to add the color to the list in the Swatches panel.

Using the Color panel

When you change the settings of a color swatch, the new settings are automatically applied to each object to which you've applied that color. However, you might want to change the color of only one object without affecting the settings of the original color swatch. You can use the Color panel to make these kinds of adjustments by applying unnamed colors.

To change an object's color by using the Color panel, follow these steps:

1 Select the object whose color you want to adjust. If a color has been applied to the object in InDesign, that color will appear in the Color panel. If the object's color was applied elsewhere, the Color panel will display the color swatch used most recently.

2 Use the tint slider or tint ramp in the Color panel to adjust the color's tint.

3 Use the panel menu to adjust the inks in Lab, CMYK, or RGB mode. (Note that after you've selected one of these, tint options are no longer available in the Color panel.) Then adjust the appropriate sliders or pick a color in the respective color spectrum.

4 To save the color as a named swatch, choose Add to Swatches from the panel menu. The color will appear as a new swatch in the Swatches panel.

Do it!

D-1: Creating custom color swatches

The files for this activity are in Student Data folder **Unit 2\Topic D**.

Here's how	Here's why
1 Open Newsletter4	
Choose **File**, **Save As**	
Edit the File name box to read **My Newsletter4**	
Click **Save**	To save the document in the current topic folder.
2 Go to page 5	The page with the Spicy Buzzard Wings recipe.
3 Using the Type tool, select the headline **Spicy Buzzard Wings**	You'll format this text with a custom color.
4 Choose **Window, Color, Color**	To open the Color panel. You'll start by creating an unnamed color, and then you'll save it as a named swatch.

5 In the top-right corner of the Color panel, click as shown

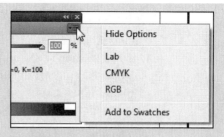

To display the panel menu.

From the panel menu, choose **CMYK**

(If necessary.) To change the color model you'll use to define the color. CMYK is used for print publishing, while RGB is used for the Web and other onscreen viewing.

The default color is black, defined as 100% black (K) and 0% of the other three color channels. You'll adjust the color channels to produce a custom green color.

6 Drag the C slider to the right to a value of **55**

To adjust the amount of cyan in the color.

Drag the Y slider to the right to a value of **45**

To adjust the amount of yellow in the color.

Drag the K slider to the left to a value of **50**

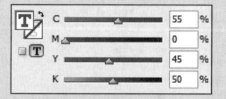

To adjust the amount of black in the color.

7 From the Color panel menu, choose **Add to Swatches**

To save the new color as a swatch.

8 Open the Swatches panel and observe the list of color swatches

(In the panel dock on the right side of the screen, click Swatches.) The color you created appears at the bottom of the list.

9 From the Swatches panel menu, choose **Swatch Options...**

To open the Swatch Options dialog box.

10 Clear **Name with Color Value**

Edit the Swatch Name box to read **Outlander Green**

Click **OK**

To rename the swatch and close the dialog box.

11 Update the document

Loading and saving swatches

Explanation

You can load swatches from documents created with Illustrator or Photoshop. You can also load swatches from other InDesign documents. In addition, you can save selected swatches in the *Adobe Swatch Exchange* (ASE) format and then load them with Illustrator or Photoshop.

To save swatches in the ASE format in InDesign, activate the Swatches panel and select the swatches you want to save. From the panel menu, choose Save Swatches. Specify a name and location for the ASE file, and click Save.

To load swatches that were saved in the ASE format, choose Load Swatches from the Swatches panel menu. Navigate to and select the ASE file you want, and click Open. All of the swatches will be loaded.

To import only selected swatches from another document, choose New Color Swatch from the Swatches panel menu. From the Color Mode list, select Other Library. Navigate to and select the desired document, and click Open. The swatches in that document will appear in the list under Color Mode. Select one or more swatches to import, and click Add to add them to the Swatches panel.

Using the Color Picker

Another way to select a custom color is to use the Color Picker. You can use the Color Picker to apply a color to the selected object or to add a custom swatch to the Swatches panel. However, the Color Picker isn't available from the Swatches panel. Instead, you can use either the Color panel or the Tools panel.

To select a color by using the Color Picker:

1 Double-click the Fill or Stroke box in either the Tools panel or the Color panel to open the Color Picker, shown in Exhibit 2-12.

2 The crosshair shows the selected color; drag in the Color Space View box to change that color. You can also enter values in the RGB, Lab, or CMYK boxes; to do so, you can type numbers in the boxes, drag the triangles in the color slider, or click in the color slider to adjust the color space along a spectrum.

3 When you have the color you want, click OK to apply it to any selected item, or click Add CMYK Swatch, Add RGB Swatch, or Add Lab Swatch (depending on the color model you're using) to add the color to the Swatches panel.

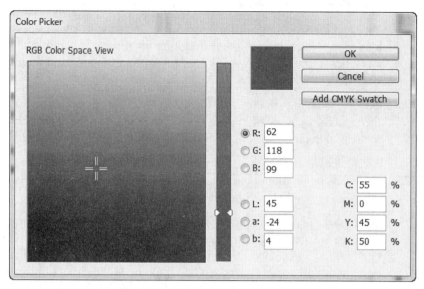

Exhibit 2-12: The Color Picker

Do it!

D-2: Loading and saving swatches

The files for this activity are in Student Data folder **Unit 2\Topic D**.

Here's how	Here's why
1 From the Swatches panel menu, choose **Load Swatches...**	To open the Open a File dialog box.
	You'll add some green color swatches that were created in another InDesign document and saved as an ASE file.
Select **Green swatches** and click **Open**	To add the swatches in the file to the Swatches panel.
2 Observe the Swatches panel	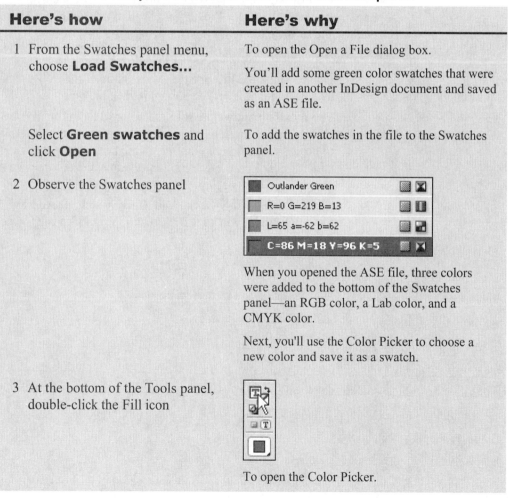
	When you opened the ASE file, three colors were added to the bottom of the Swatches panel—an RGB color, a Lab color, and a CMYK color.
	Next, you'll use the Color Picker to choose a new color and save it as a swatch.
3 At the bottom of the Tools panel, double-click the Fill icon	
	To open the Color Picker.

4 Click anywhere in the green area of the RGB Color Space View box	To select a new green color.
Click **Add CMYK Swatch**	To add the color to the Swatches panel.
Click **OK**	To close the Color Picker.
5 In the Swatches panel, verify that the color you created is selected	The swatch is named with the CMYK values of the color you picked. You'll create an ASE file that includes the color you just created.
6 Press (SHIFT) and click the color **Outlander Green**	To select the bottom five colors in the Swatches panel—the three you loaded plus the two you created.
7 From the Swatches panel menu, choose **Save Swatches...**	To open the Save As dialog box.
Edit the File name box to read **My green swatches**	You'll save the five color swatches so that other people can load them into their Adobe CS5 applications.
In the Save as type list, verify that **Adobe Swatch Exchange** is selected	
Navigate to the current topic folder and click **Save**	To save the set of swatches as an ASE file.
8 Close the Swatches panel	
9 Close the Color panel	
10 Update and close the document	

Unit summary: Basic documents

Topic A　　In this topic, you learned how to **create a document** and how to create a document preset.

Topic B　　In this topic, you learned how to **create text** in InDesign and how to place text from another file. You also learned how to apply basic **character formatting**.

Topic C　　In this topic, you learned how to place **graphics** in a document, including placing pages from other InDesign documents as graphics.

Topic D　　In this topic, you learned about the difference between named color swatches in the **Swatches panel** and unnamed colors in the **Color panel**. You created custom color swatches, and you loaded and saved custom swatches.

Independent practice activity

In this activity, you'll create a document, add and format text, and place text. You'll also create a custom color, and you'll place and position graphics.

1　Create a one-page, single-column document. Set the margins as follows: Top margin, 12p0; Bottom, Left, and Right margins, 3p0.

2　Save the document as **My note** in the Unit summary folder for this unit.

3　At the top margin guide, create a text frame and type **Note from the President**. Format the text as Trebuchet MS, bold italic, 46 point.

4　Resize the text frame so that all the text fits on one line and the frame fits the contents. Align the text frame with the top, left, and right margin guides, as shown in Exhibit 2-13. Deselect the text frame.

5　Create a color swatch of your choice. Name the color **My outlander color**. Apply the new color to the heading text.

6　Place the President picture, located in the Images folder. (*Hint:* In the Place dialog box, clear Show Import Options.)

7　Place the Note document. Adjust the text frame as necessary so that all the text is visible.

8　Insert the three small spice graphics: Cinnamon, Coriander, and Nutmeg. They are located in the Images folder.

9　Position and resize the elements as shown in Exhibit 2-13.

10　Update and close the document.

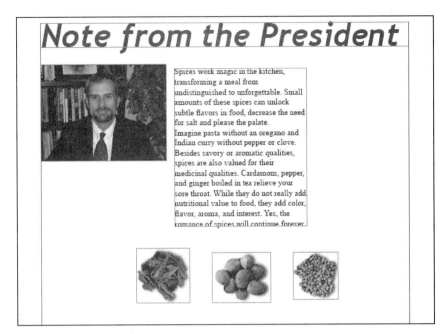

Exhibit 2-13: The My note document after Step 9

Review questions

1 You want to create a document for a magazine layout with left- and right-facing pages. In the New Document dialog box, which of the following should you do?

A Check Facing Pages.

B Select an option from the Page Size list.

C Select a landscape orientation.

D Enter values in the Bleed and Slug boxes.

2 You find that you're frequently creating blank documents with the same custom settings. What is the most efficient way to save and access these settings?

A Create a document preset.

B Copy and paste objects from an existing document.

C Open an existing document, choose File, Save As to save it as a document with a different name, and delete the unnecessary content.

D Manually enter the settings in the New Document dialog box each time you create a document.

3 Using the Type tool, you drag in a layout to create a text frame. Before doing anything else, you choose File, Place to place a text document. When you select the document and click Open, what happens?

A InDesign creates a new, separate text frame with the placed text.

B InDesign prompts you to choose where you want to place the text.

C InDesign loads the text into the pointer.

D InDesign places the text in the text frame you just created.

4 To create a text frame:

A Double-click the Type tool.

B Double-click the Selection tool.

C Drag the Type tool.

D Drag the Rectangle tool.

5 Using the Rectangle Frame tool, you drag in a layout to create a frame. Before doing anything else, you choose File, Place to place a graphics file. When you select the file and click Open, what happens?

A InDesign creates a new, separate frame with the placed graphic.

B InDesign prompts you to choose where you want to place the graphic.

C InDesign loads the graphic into the pointer.

D InDesign places the graphic in the frame you just created.

6 You've created an InDesign document that contains a layout page you'll need to update frequently. You want to use this layout in several documents. How can you do this most efficiently, so that the layout will update in each document when you edit the original?

A Whenever you edit the document, copy and paste it into other documents as desired.

B Place the document page in the other documents as you would a graphic.

C Use master pages.

D You can't place InDesign pages in other documents.

7 You've created a custom color swatch. How can you save it for use in an Adobe Illustrator document?

A Drag the swatch to the Illustrator document.

B Copy and paste the swatch.

C From the Swatches panel menu, choose Duplicate Swatch.

D From the Swatches panel menu, choose Save Swatches.

8 You want to change the color settings for an object to which you've previously applied a named swatch, but you don't want to change the settings for other objects that use the same swatch. Which panel should you use to do this most efficiently?

A The Swatches panel

B The Color panel

C The Paragraph Styles panel

D The Info panel

Unit 3

Guides and master pages

Unit time: 45 minutes

Complete this unit, and you'll know how to:

A Position elements precisely by using guides and the Control panel.

B Create master pages and apply them to a document.

Topic A: Object positioning

This topic covers the following ACE exam objective for InDesign CS5.

#	Objective
1.11	Describe the use of Smart Guides.

Precise positioning

Explanation

Some designers use the "eyeball" method to place objects in a layout, arranging them until they look good to the eye. But you'll probably find that you can achieve greater consistency—and ultimately save time—by using ruler guides, smart guides, and the Control panel to align or position objects precisely.

Ruler guides

To create ruler guides, drag from the horizontal and vertical rulers onto a document page. If you place a guide on a page, the guide extends only to the edges of the page. If you place a guide on the pasteboard, the guide extends across the document window. To align items to a guide, using the Selection tool, drag the item so that it snaps to the guide. You can also use the arrow keys to nudge items into position.

You can manually place ruler guides in a layout, but the layout might call for many evenly spaced guides, and adding these manually would be tedious. Instead, you can have InDesign create them.

To create a set of evenly spaced ruler guides:

1   Choose Layout, Create Guides to open the Create Guides dialog box.
2   Specify the number of rows and/or columns you want in the layout.
3   Specify whether you want a gutter between the rows and/or columns.
4   Under Options, select either Margins or Page to specify the reference point for the guides.
5   Check Remove Existing Ruler Guides to clear any guides currently in the layout.
6   Check Preview and verify that the guides are placed correctly.
7   Click OK.

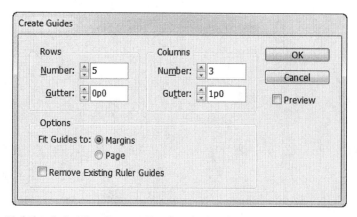

Exhibit 3-1: The Create Guides dialog box

Sometimes it helps to preview the page without guides showing. To temporarily hide or show guides, choose View, Grids & Guides, and choose either Hide Guides or Show Guides. (This option is also available from the View Options menu.) You can also use the keyboard shortcut Ctrl+; to hide or show guides, or you can switch to the Preview screen mode.

Smart guides

Smart guides become immediately obvious whenever you move an object in a layout. InDesign provides information about the object's size, location, and alignment with the page and with other objects in the layout.

When you move an object, for example, a gray box appears next to the mouse pointer; the box shows X and Y coordinates, indicating the location of the object's reference point. (Note that these coordinates are not the location of the mouse pointer—that information can be found in the Info panel.) Similarly, when you resize an object, the "smart cursor" shows W and H dimensions for the object. This way, you don't have to take your eyes off the layout to watch the Control panel as you're manipulating objects.

Smart guides also indicate how layout objects are aligned. As you drag objects, guides appear, indicating when an object's center or edges are aligned with the center of a column, the center of the page, or the center or edges of other objects. Furthermore, if you have more than two objects in a layout, smart guides indicate even spacing between the objects.

Although useful, smart guides can sometimes get in the way as you're arranging objects. If you have many objects in a layout, for example, multiple smart guides might appear whenever you make an adjustment. One solution to this problem is to zoom in on the area you're working with, because smart guides indicate alignment only with objects currently in view.

Another solution is to change the preferences for smart guides, shown in Exhibit 3-2. To do so, choose Edit, Preferences, Guides & Pasteboard. Under Smart Guide Options, check or clear the desired options. Also, you can turn smart guides off by choosing View, Grids & Guides, Smart Guides (also available from the View Options menu).

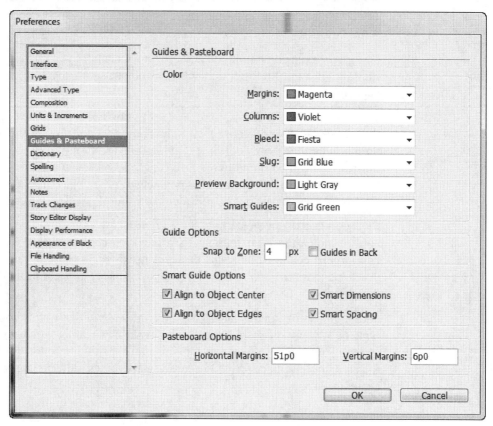

Exhibit 3-2: Smart Guide options

Do it!

A-1:   Aligning elements to guides

The files for this activity are in Student Data folder **Unit 3\Topic A**.

Here's how	Here's why
1 Open Guides	
Choose **File, Save As...**	
Edit the File name box to read **My guides**	
Click **Save**	
2 Go to page 5	If necessary.
3 Deselect all page elements	(If necessary.) Click a blank area of the page or pasteboard.
4 Point to the horizontal ruler, click, and hold	(At the top of the document window.) The pointer changes to a two-headed arrow.
Slowly drag down onto page 5	(Don't release the mouse button.) To create a guide.
Observe the Y value as you drag	(Next to the pointer.) The smart cursor shows the vertical location of the guide in the layout.
Drag the guide onto the page and release the mouse button	
5 In the Control panel, edit the Y Location box to read **18**	
Press (↵ ENTER)	To position the ruler guide at 18p0 on the vertical ruler.
6 Using the Selection tool, position the two text frames so that their top edges align with the ruler guide	
7 Update the document	

Using the Control panel

Explanation

You can position elements by using specific values. To do this, select an object and enter values in the X and Y Location boxes in the Control panel, shown in Exhibit 3-3. By clicking the Reference Point locator in the Control panel, you can position an object relative to its corners, sides, or center. The X-coordinate positions the text frame or graphics frame based on a position on the horizontal ruler, and the Y-coordinate positions the frame based on a position on the vertical ruler. For example, if you want to place the top-left corner of a selected frame at the 30p0 mark on the horizontal ruler, select the top-left corner of the Reference Point locator, type 30 in the X Location box, and press Enter.

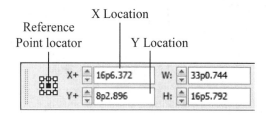

Exhibit 3-3: The Control panel shows an object's position

Do it!

A-2: Precisely positioning elements by using the Control panel and smart guides

Here's how	Here's why
1 Drag the Nutmeg graphic approximately as shown	**Wings**
	Method
	(Previously, you placed this on the pasteboard.) Align the graphic's right edge with the right page margin, and place the graphic between the recipe name and the instructions.
	As you place the graphic, notice the smart guides indicating even spacing between the heading above and the text box below the graphic.
2 In the Control panel, select the center reference point	X: 95p5 Y: 13p1.272
	If necessary.
Observe the X Location and Y Location boxes	You'll align the three graphics so that their centers are aligned horizontally and are evenly spaced.
Edit the Y Location box to read **13** and press ⏎ ENTER	

3 Select the Cinnamon graphic

Edit the X Location box to read **85p5** and press (TAB)

To space the graphic's center point 10 picas to the left of the Nutmeg graphic.

Edit the Y Location box to read **13** and press (↵ ENTER)

To horizontally align the graphic's center point with the center point of the Nutmeg graphic.

4 Select the Coriander graphic

You'll align this graphic with the other two spice graphics and space them evenly by using smart guides.

Begin dragging the Coriander graphic to the left of the Cinnamon graphic

To see that smart guides indicate when the graphic is aligned with the center point and edges of the Cinnamon graphic.

Drag the graphic until the smart guides indicate even spacing and alignment with center points, as shown

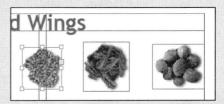

The smart guides will indicate when the image is horizontally centered with the other two graphics and vertically centered in the column gutter.

5 Update and close the document

Topic B: Master pages

This topic covers the following ACE exam objectives for InDesign CS5.

#	Objective
1.3	Given a scenario, work with master pages.
2.1	Insert special characters by using the Type menu, Glyph panel, or context menu.
4.1	Given a scenario, determine the best settings for choosing and placing an image.

Using master pages

Explanation

Most publications have some features that are common to all pages. For example, magazines usually have the title of the magazine and a page number on every page. A *master page* acts as a template for pages in a document. Any items on a master page will automatically be added to pages in the document that have the master page applied.

Each new document is created with a default master page titled A-Master, which is in the master page section of the Pages panel, shown in Exhibit 3-4. This master page contains the margin and column settings you specified in the New Document dialog box when you created the document.

To change the guides on the default master page, or to add items to it, double-click the master-page icon to display the master page in the document window. Then choose Layout, Margins and Columns to open the Margins and Columns dialog box. You can then enter values in the Margins or Columns boxes. Column guides divide pages into vertical sections so that you can create evenly spaced columns of text. The Gutter value denotes the space between columns.

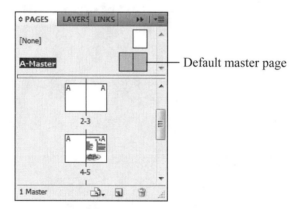

Default master page

Exhibit 3-4: A document with a single master page applied to it

Renaming master pages

By default, new master pages are named alphabetically. For example, new master pages are named B-Master, C-Master, and so on. You might want to give them descriptive names instead. To rename a master page, choose Master Options for "*<master page name>*" from the Pages panel menu and enter a new name in the Master Options dialog box. The new name must still retain a prefix (up to four characters), but it will also include the name you specified. For example, you could rename the default master page as "#12A-Front page."

Do it! **B-1: Editing the default master page**

The files for this activity are in Student Data folder **Unit 3\Topic B**.

Here's how	Here's why
1 Open Masters	
Save the publication as **My masters**	
2 Open the Pages panel	
Observe the master page section	There are two master-page spreads available by default. However, you cannot modify the None master. By default, all pages in a document use the A-Master.
3 Double-click the text **A-Master**, as shown	
	To display the A-master spread in the document window. Both the left- and right-page icons should be highlighted.
4 Point to the horizontal ruler, click, and hold	
Begin dragging down onto the left master page	
Press and hold (CTRL)	To apply the horizontal ruler guide to the entire spread.
Drag the guide to 5p0 on the vertical ruler	
5 Press (CTRL) + (D)	To open the Place dialog box.
Clear **Show Import Options**	If necessary.
Navigate to the Images folder	In the Common folder.
Double-click **Left banner**	

6	Click on the layout	To place the graphic.
	Position the graphic on the left master page as shown	

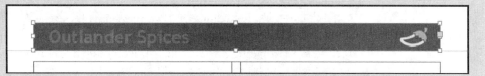

		Position the graphic so that its bottom edge aligns with the ruler guide you created, and its left and right edges align with the page margins.
	Deselect the graphic	
7	Open the Place dialog box	
	Select **Right banner**	
	Check **Show Import Options** and click **Open**	To open the Image Import Options dialog box.
8	Click the **Layers** tab	
	Click the eye icon to the left of Pepper	

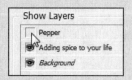

		To hide the Pepper layer.
	Click **OK**	
9	Click on the layout	
	Position the graphic on the right master page as shown	

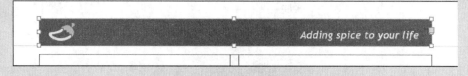

10	From the Pages panel menu, choose **Master Options for "A-Master"...**	To open the Master Options dialog box.
	Edit the Name box to read **2col**	
	Click **OK**	To close the dialog box.
11	Update the document	

Inserting page numbers

Explanation

To insert automatic page numbers, display the desired master page and place the insertion point in a text frame. Choose Type, Insert Special Character, Markers, and choose a page number option: Current Page Number, Next Page Number, Previous Page Number, Section Marker, or Footnote Number. (You can also right-click to insert special characters by using the shortcut menu.) Insert any text that you want to accompany the page number, such as the publication name or a section indicator. For document with facing pages, you will likely add a text frame with one of these special characters to both the left and right pages of the master spread.

All pages based on the master page will then display the page number. If you add, delete, or rearrange pages, InDesign renumbers them automatically.

Locking master-page objects

If you want to prevent objects on the master page from being edited or accidentally deleted in the document, then you can lock them so they can't be overridden. On the master mage, first select the objects that you want to lock. Then, from the Pages panel menu, choose Allow Master Item Overrides on Selection to clear it. (If this option is checked, the selected object can be overridden in the document.)

Do it!

B-2:   Inserting page numbers

Here's how	Here's why
1 Create a horizontal ruler guide at 62p0 that spans the entire spread	Point to the horizontal ruler, click, and hold. Press Ctrl and drag the guide to the 62p0 mark on the vertical ruler.
	You'll include automatic page numbers on each page of the document except the front and back pages. First, you'll create automatic page numbers for the left pages.
2 Click the Type tool	
On the left page, create a text frame that is approximately 2p0 high and aligns with the left and right margin guides	
3 Press CTRL + 2	(If necessary.) To zoom in on the new text frame.
4 Choose **Type**, **Insert Special Character**, **Markers**, **Current Page Number**	
	To insert the current-page-number character, which appears as the letter A on this master page, corresponding to the master page's prefix.
5 In the Control panel, click as shown	
	(If necessary.) The Paragraph Formatting Tools button.
In the Control panel, click	(The "Align away from spine" button.) You'll duplicate this text frame on the right-side page; this alignment option will automatically move the text to the outside margin.
6 Display the entire page in the document window	You will now duplicate the character for the right master page.

7	Click the Selection tool	The text frame is now selected.
	Begin dragging the text frame to the right	You'll copy the frame as you drag it.
	Press and hold (SHIFT) + (ALT)	Holding Shift constrains the object's movement, and holding Alt duplicates the object.
	Drag the text frame so it aligns with the left and right margins on the right page	
8	Observe the page number marker on the right page	To verify that it is aligned away from the document spine.
9	Press (CTRL) + (A)	To select all of the objects in the layout. You want to lock the objects on this page so that they can't be overridden.
	From the Pages panel menu, choose **Allow Master Item Overrides on Selection**	To deselect this option.
10	Update the document	

Creating master pages

Explanation

For most complex documents, you'll need more than one master page. You can create many master pages, each designed to specify layout elements for one or more document pages. To create a new master page, choose New Master from the Pages panel menu to open the New Master dialog box. If you have multiple master pages, you can enter a custom name and prefix for the new master.

Parent and child master pages

You can base a master page on another master page or create a master page from an existing layout page. For example, if you want certain objects to appear on every page of a document, you can place them on a master page. However, you might want to have several master-page layouts in a document, all of which use some common elements. You can create one master—the *parent master*—that contains some basic objects, such as automatic page numbers, a logo, or whatever you'd like to print on each document page. Then you can create *child master* pages that have different objects on them.

The child masters contain any objects you place on the parent master, and the child master pages are updated when you update the parent. However, objects on a child master page appear only on pages to which the child master is applied. The relationship might look something like that shown in Exhibit 3-5.

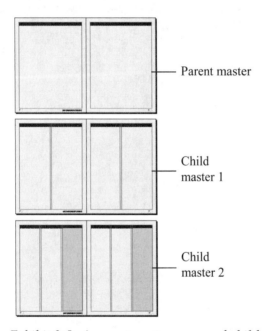

Exhibit 3-5: A parent master page and child master pages

To base a new master on an existing master:

1 From the Pages panel menu, choose New Master to open the New Master dialog box.

2 From the Based on Master list, select a master page to be the parent.

3 Click OK.

To make an existing master the child of another master:

1 Go to the master page that you want to turn into a child master.

2 From the Pages panel menu, choose Master Options for "*<master page name>*" to open the Master Options dialog box.

3 From the Based on Master list, select the master you want to use as the parent.

4 Click OK.

Loading master pages

To load all master pages from one document into another, choose Load Master Pages from the Pages panel menu. In the Open a File dialog box, select the document containing the masters you want to import and click Open. All of the master pages in the source document are loaded into the active document.

Creating masters based on layouts

Another way to create master pages is to base them on existing layouts. You'll often design a layout before you know specifically how you want it to look or what elements to include. Once you've got it the way you want it, you can save it as a master. To do so, first make sure the spread you want to save is selected. (You can save only whole spreads as masters.) Then, from the Pages panel menu, choose Save as Master to create a new master. If the layout was based on an existing master page, then the master you create from it will be a child of that master.

Do it!

B-3: Creating new master pages

Here's how	Here's why
1 From the Pages panel menu, choose **New Master...**	To open the New Master dialog box.
Edit the Name box to read **3-col**	
From the Based on Master list, select **A-2col**	
Click **OK**	To create the new master, which appears in the Pages panel below the A-2-col master.
2 Observe the Pages panel	

	The new master's icon indicates that it's a child of the A master. Therefore, it includes all of the elements on the A-2-col master you created. The page number markers have changed to reflect the new master page's prefix.
	You want this master to have a three-column layout.
3 Choose **Layout, Margins and Columns...**	To open the Margins and Columns dialog box.
Set the number of columns to **3**, and verify that the gutter width is set to **1p0**	
Click **OK**	To close the dialog box and apply the changes.
	Next, you'll load some master pages from another document.
4 From the Pages panel menu, choose **Load Master Pages...**	To open the Open a File dialog box.
Select the **Load masters** document and click **Open**	(From the current topic folder.) To load the master pages from the document.
5 Observe the Pages panel	

You've added two new master spreads, C-Cover 1 and D-Cover 4.

6 Double-click **C-Cover 1**

To display the master page. It includes graphics, ruler guides, and several frames used as placeholders.

Next, you'll create a master based on an existing spread.

7 Display the pages 4-5 spread

In the Pages panel, click 4-5 under the spread thumbnail.

8 From the Pages panel menu, choose **Save as Master**

To save the spread as a new master, A-Master.

Although you can save only spreads as masters (rather than individual pages from a spread), you can delete pages from a master spread.

9 In the Pages panel, double-click the left-page thumbnail of A-Master

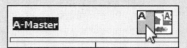

To select the left-facing page of the master you just created.

   From the Pages panel menu, choose **Delete Master Page**

10 From the Pages panel menu, choose **Master Options for "A-Master"...**

   Edit the Prefix box to read **R**

You'll use the prefix "R" to indicate a recipe spread.

   Edit the Name box to read **Recipe**

   Observe the Based on Master list

The spread is a child of the A-2-col master.

   Click **OK**

11 Update the document

Applying master pages

Explanation

To apply a master page to a document page, drag the master-page icon from the master pages section in the Pages panel and place it directly on a page icon in the document pages section. The page icon will change to show that the master page has been applied, as shown in Exhibit 3-6.

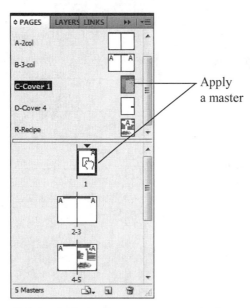

Exhibit 3-6: Applying master pages by using the Pages panel

You can also use the Pages panel menu to specify a range or selection of pages to apply a master page to. From the Pages panel menu, choose Apply Master to Pages to open the Apply Master dialog box. Select a master from the Apply Master list, and then enter the page range or selections (page numbers separated by commas) in the To Pages box.

Do it!

B-4: Applying master pages

Here's how	Here's why
1 Go to page 1	You want the first page of the document to use the C-Cover 1 master page.
2 Fit the entire page in the document window	If necessary.
Observe the Pages panel	Page 2 has the A master applied to it.
3 Drag the C-Cover 1 icon to the Page 1 thumbnail, as shown	

C-Cover 1
D-Cover 4

The first page in the document now contains all of the objects on the master page.

Next, you'll add the B-3-col master spread to multiple pages at once.

4 Go to page 2	
5 Right-click anywhere in the Pages panel	To display the shortcut menu.
Choose **Apply Master to Pages…**	To open the Apply Master dialog box.
6 From the Apply Master list, select **B-3-col**	

Apply Master

Apply Master: B-3-col
To Pages: 2,6

In the To Pages box, enter **2,6**

To apply the master spread to pages 2 and 6.

Click **OK**	Pages 2 and 6 now use the B master.
7 Observe the bottom of page 2	The correct page number appears because you inserted the Current Page Number marker on the master.
8 Drag the D-Cover 4 master to the Page 8 thumbnail	To apply the master to page 8.
9 Drag the R-Recipe master to the Page 5 thumbnail	
10 Update the document	

Modifying master-page items

Explanation
You can modify master-page items on the master pages. But you might need to modify the master items on a single document page or spread without changing the look of the master items on the rest of the pages in your document.

To override all of the master-page items on an individual document page or spread without changing the master page itself:

1　In the Pages panel, select the page icons for the pages containing the master-page items you want to modify.

- To select multiple pages that aren't continuous, click the first page icon to select it; then press Ctrl and click each additional page icon you want to select.

- To select multiple continuous pages, click the first page icon you want to select; then press Shift and click the last page you want to select. The two pages you clicked and all pages between them will be selected.

- To select a spread, click the page numbers below the page icons for that spread.

2　From the Pages panel menu, choose Override All Master Page Items.

3　Delete, move, or edit the master-page items.

If you want to reset the selected pages to again display the locked master-page items with their original appearance, then choose Remove All Local Overrides from the Pages panel menu. (Choose Remove Selected Local Overrides for only the currently selected master-page item.)

Of course, you might want to modify only one or two objects from the master page. To do so, press Ctrl+Shift and click the master-page object you want to override. You can also override frames that appear on the master page by placing text or graphics into them. To do so, load the text or graphics into the pointer and click the frame to place the content.

When you use either of the above techniques to override master-page objects, the objects retain a link to the master page. You can modify them as you wish, but any attributes (such as fill, stroke, or size) you don't modify will update if you adjust them on the master page. To completely sever the link between an object and its master page, first override the desired objects or pages. Then, from the Pages panel menu, choose either Detach Selection from Master or Detach All Objects from Master.

Do it!

B-5: Overriding a master-page object on a document page

The files for this activity are in Student Data folder **Unit 3\Topic B**.

Here's how	Here's why
1 Go to page 1	You want to use the placeholders on the master page to insert text and graphics.
2 Using the Selection tool, try to select any object on the page	Because these items are on a master page, you can't select them without first overriding them.
3 Press ⟨CTRL⟩ + ⟨SHIFT⟩ and click the frame in the right column	
4 Press ⟨CTRL⟩ + ⟨D⟩	To open the Place dialog box.
Select **Bay leaves spice**	From the Images folder.
Clear **Show Import Options**	If necessary.
Click **Open**	To load the image into the pointer.
5 Observe the graphics frame	The image is placed but it is too large for the frame.
6 Choose **Edit**, **Undo Replace**	To reload the mouse pointer.
7 In the Control panel, check **Auto-Fit**	
Click in the graphics frame	To place the fitted image in it.
8 Observe the graphics frame	
9 Press ⟨CTRL⟩ + ⟨SHIFT⟩ and click in the column to the left of the graphics placeholder	There is a text frame here that you want to override.
10 Place the document **Cover story** in the selected text frame	From the current topic folder.
11 Update and close the document	

Unit summary: Guides and master pages

Topic A   In this topic, you learned how to position objects precisely by using **guides**, the Control panel, and smart guides.

Topic B   In this topic, you worked with **master pages**. You learned how to create and edit master pages and add **automatic page numbers** to them. You also learned how to apply master pages to document pages and how to **override** master-page objects.

Independent practice activity

In this activity, you'll arrange objects in a layout by using guides and the Control panel. Then you'll create and apply master pages.

The files for this activity are in Student Data folder **Unit 3\Unit summary**.

1 Open Guides and masters practice.

2 Save the document as **My guides and masters practice**.

3 Save the spread as a new master.

4 On the master, align the President photo to the horizontal ruler guide at 17p0.

5 Align the Nutmeg graphic to the 17p0 ruler guide and the right page margin, as shown in Exhibit 3-7.

6 Using the Control panel, position the Cinnamon graphic so that its center point is aligned vertically with that of the Nutmeg graphic and is 8 picas below it. (*Hint:* The top of the Nutmeg graphic is aligned at 17p0. Select the Cinnamon graphic; then select its top-center reference point to position it vertically below the Nutmeg graphic.)

7 Using smart guides, position the Coriander graphic so that its center point is aligned vertically with that of the Cinnamon graphic and is 8 picas below it. (*Hint:* Zoom in on the three spice graphics.)

8 Using smart guides, align the text frame to the 17p0 ruler guide, evenly spaced between the President and Nutmeg graphics so that the master appears as shown in Exhibit 3-8.

9 Go to page 1. Press Ctrl+A, and then press Delete to delete everything on the page.

10 Apply the master to page 1.

11 Update and close the document.

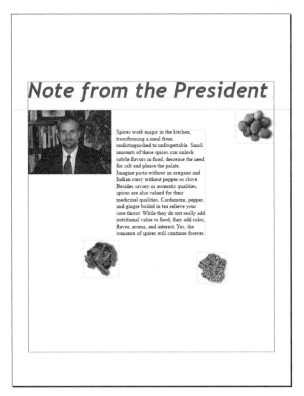

Exhibit 3-7: The new master page after Step 5

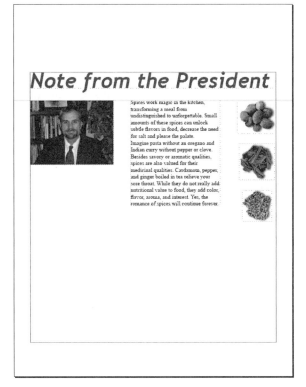

Exhibit 3-8: The master page after Step 8

Review questions

1 How can you add a guide to a document page at a specific horizontal or vertical position?

   A Choose View, Grids & Guides, Show Guides.

   B Press Ctrl+semi-colon.

   C Drag from the horizontal or vertical ruler.

   D Choose Edit, Preferences, Grids & Pasteboard, and check Guides in Back.

2 For which of the following scenarios would smart guides be helpful? [Choose all that apply.]

   A You want to align the edges of two objects.

   B You want to space three objects equal distances from one another.

   C You want to observe the X and Y dimensions of an object's center point as you drag it.

   D You want to create a series of evenly spaced ruler guides.

3 You want to use different layouts for different pages in a document, so that pages with similar layouts have guides and objects in common. You also want to be able to update each layout and have changes apply to similar pages. What is the most efficient way to accomplish this?

   A Copy and paste objects, and adjust individual page settings.

   B Create separate documents for each different layout.

   C Create a different master page or spread for each different layout.

   D Create one master page, and then override master items as necessary.

4 You have a 10-page document with one master page applied to all 10 pages. The master page contains common elements, including the company logo. On page 4, you want to delete only the logo, but you want it to remain on the other nine pages. After you go to page 4, what is the next step?

   A Select the object on the document page.

   B Press Ctrl+Shift and click the logo.

   C Delete the object from the master page.

   D Delete the master page.

5 True or false? To automatically fit an image to a graphics frame when you place it, you must check Auto-Size first.

6 You want to automatically insert the page number on each page of the document so that if you rearrange pages later, the numbering will still be accurate. You should:

   A Create a text frame on each page and enter the page number.

   B Insert the Current Page Number special character on each master page.

   C Do nothing—InDesign does this automatically.

   D Set this option in Preferences.

Unit 4

Typesetting

Unit time: 90 minutes

Complete this unit, and you'll know how to:

A Thread text between text frames, add jump lines, and change the number of columns in a text frame.

B Use the Paragraph Formatting Controls to apply paragraph formatting, and use Find/Change to replace formatting.

C Create and edit paragraph and character styles.

Topic A: Text frame threading

This topic covers the following ACE exam objectives for InDesign CS5.

#	Objective
2.3	Adjust the look of text inside a text frame by using Text Frame Options.
2.4	Given a scenario, set a paragraph to span more than one text column or split into multiple sub-columns.
2.5	Manipulate text flow by using text threading, smart text reflow, resizing, and text wrap.

Flowing text between text frames

Explanation

Multiple-page documents often contain one or more stories that begin in one text frame and continue into other text frames on the same page or on other pages. You can use InDesign to control how text flows among text frames.

Threading text frames

When you place text into a text frame, the frame might not be big enough to display all of the text. When this occurs, a red plus sign appears near the lower-right corner of the frame, indicating overset text. When text won't fit in a single text frame, you can flow the text into additional text frames and then link the original frame to the other frames, as shown in Exhibit 4-1. This process is called *threading* text.

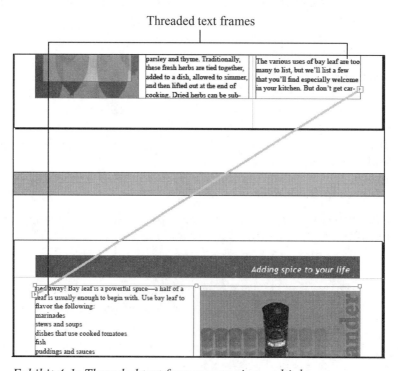

Exhibit 4-1: Threaded text frames spanning multiple pages

To thread text:

1 With the Selection tool, click the first text frame that contains overset text.

2 Thread the text to an existing frame, or create a new text frame.

- To thread the text to an existing text frame, click the red plus sign at the bottom of the first text frame, and then click the text frame into which you want to thread the text. (The pointer changes to an arrow and two interlocking links to indicate that these frames will be linked.)

- To create a new text frame, click the red plus sign at the bottom of the first text frame; then either click a blank area of the page or drag to create a new text frame.

3 If you need to thread the text into additional text frames, use one of the following methods:

- **Manual text flow** — Thread the text manually into each additional text frame, as described in Step 2.

- **Semi-autoflow** — Press Alt while clicking the red plus sign at the bottom of a text frame, and click or drag to create a new text frame. The pointer automatically reloads any remaining overset text, so you can thread additional text frames without clicking the red plus sign each time.

- **Autoflow** — Press Shift and click to automatically add frames and pages until all available text has flowed into the document. This method is useful if you have a lot of text in a document, such as a book.

- **Fixed-page autoflow** — Press Shift+Alt and click to flow text into the existing pages of the document without adding more pages.

4 To see which text frames are threaded, choose View, Show Text Threads, and click a threaded text frame with the Selection tool. Lines connect the bottom-right and top-left corners of threaded frames.

Smart Text Reflow

Another option for flowing text as you type is to use Smart Text Reflow. By default, when you're typing in a frame linked to a master page and you come to the end of the frame, InDesign adds a new page at the end of the story. In order for this feature to be active, though, a text frame must be threaded to at least one other text frame on a different page. You can specify preferences for Smart Text Reflow by choosing Edit, Preferences, Type.

Unthreading text frames

After you have threaded text frames across pages, you might need to break the links and flow the text through other text frames. To unthread text frames:

1 Select one of the threaded text frames to show the lines representing the text flow. A blue arrowhead appears at either the bottom-right or top-left corner of the threaded text frame to represent text flowing out of or into the frame.

2 Double-click the arrowhead in either text frame. The pointer changes to a chain link with one broken link.

3 Click the frame you want to unthread. The link breaks, and the text flows to fill other threaded text frames (if any).

You can also click a text frame with the Selection tool and press Delete to delete the entire text frame. No text is deleted with either method.

Do it!

A-1: Threading text

The files for this activity are in Student Data folder **Unit 4\Topic A**.

Here's how	Here's why
1 Open Typesetting Save the document as **My typesetting**	A story has been placed in the text frame on page 1, but it's too long to fit. You'll thread it to another text box on a different page.
2 Go to page 1	If necessary.
Zoom in	If necessary.
3 Using the Selection tool, click anywhere on the two-column text frame	To select it. The text frame contains the story under the heading "Spices of the month."
Observe the bottom-right corner of the text frame	The various uses of bay leaf are too many to list, but we'll list a few that you'll find especially welcome in your kitchen. But don't get car- A small red plus sign appears, indicating overset text.
4 Using the Selection tool, click the red plus sign	To load the overset text into the pointer. You will create a new text frame in which to thread this story.
5 Go to page 3	This page contains a text frame that spans both columns.
6 Point to the left column	The pointer changes to a link icon to indicate that you are pointing to a frame to which you can link the loaded text.
Click the text frame	To thread the two text frames. The text flows into the frame you clicked, and another small red plus sign appears at the bottom-right corner.
7 Choose **View, Extras, Show Text Threads**	To display a blue line that indicates the direction of text flow between threaded frames.
8 Press [H]	To temporarily select the Hand tool.
Drag up	To see the bottom of page 1 and the top of page 3. The text thread flows from the bottom of the text frame on page 1 to the top of the text frame on page 3.
9 Choose **View, Extras, Hide Text Threads**	
10 Update the document	

Multiple-column text frames

Explanation   Most documents produced with a word-processing program contain a single column of text that spans the page. One thing you can do to make your document look more professional is to convert page-spanning columns into multiple columns, as in newspapers and magazines. You can resize the single column and then thread the overset text into another text frame, but there is an easier way. You can add multiple columns to a single text frame.

To add columns to a text frame:

1 Select the text frame with the Selection tool.
2 Choose Object, Text Frame Options to open the Text Frame Options dialog box.
3 Under Columns, enter the desired number of columns.
4 Specify the desired settings:
    • Enter the width of each column.
    • Check Fixed Column Width if you want to maintain the column widths you specify even if you subsequently resize the frame.
    • Check Balance Columns if you want to balance text across multiple columns within a text frame.
5 Enter a value for the gutter.
6 Click OK.

Using this method will produce columns of equal widths. If your design requires adjacent columns with different widths, you can create separate text frames and thread the text.

Another way to make adjustments to columns in a text frame is to use the tools in the Control panel, as shown in Exhibit 4-2:

• In the Number of Columns box, enter the desired number of columns.

• In the Gutter box, enter a value for the space between columns.

• Unbalanced Columns is selected by default. Click Balance Columns to balance the text across multiple columns.

• Set the vertical alignment by selecting Align top, Align center, Align bottom, or Justify vertically.

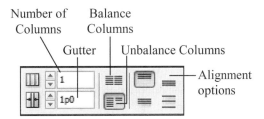

Exhibit 4-2: Text frame tools in the Control panel

Spanning columns

After adding multiple columns to a single text frame, you can set a paragraph to span the columns, such as for a headline that spans a three-column article.

1 Place the insertion point in the paragraph.

2 From the Control panel menu or the Paragraph panel menu, choose Span Columns to open Span Columns dialog box, shown in Exhibit 4-22.

3 From the Paragraph Layout list, select Span Columns.

4 In the Span box, select the number of columns the paragraph will span.

5 In the Space Before Span and Space After Span boxes, enter the desired spacing values.

6 Click OK.

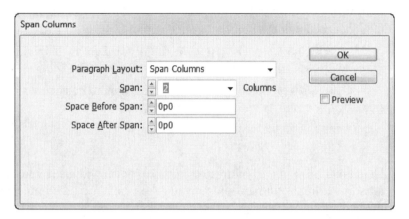

Exhibit 4-3: The Span Columns dialog box with Span Columns selected in the Paragraph Layout list

Splitting paragraphs into columns

You can also split a paragraph into multiple columns within a text frame. For example, let's say you are laying out a recipe card and all the text is contained in a one-column text frame. To make the list of ingredients stand out, you've decided to split the list into two columns while leaving the text above and below the ingredients in one column. Here's how you'd do it:

1 Place the insertion point in the desired paragraph or select the desired paragraphs.

2 From the Control panel menu or the Paragraph panel menu, choose Span Columns to open Span Columns dialog box.

3 From the Paragraph Layout list, select Split Columns.

4 In the Sub-columns box, enter the number of columns the paragraph will split into, as shown in Exhibit 4-4.

5 In the Space Before Split and Space After Split boxes, enter the desired spacing values. In the Inside Gutter and Outside Gutter boxes, set the gutter spacing.

6 Click OK.

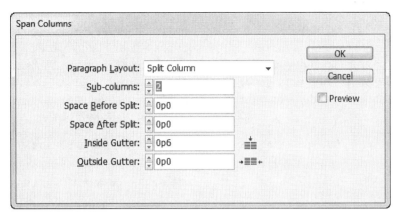

Exhibit 4-4: The Span Columns dialog box with Split Columns selected in the Paragraph Layout list

Do it!

A-2:   Adding columns to a text frame

Here's how	Here's why
1 Go to page 3	(If necessary.) The text frame contains one column that spans the page. You'll format the text frame to have two columns.
2 Choose **Object**, **Text Frame Options...**	To open the Text Frame Options dialog box.
3 Under Columns, edit the Number box to read **2**	The value in the Width box changes automatically to compensate for the number of columns and the gutter between them.
Click **OK**	To apply the changes. The text frame now contains two columns. In addition, formatting the frame with two columns rather than one has caused the text to re-flow so that it fits.
4 Update the document	

Jump-line page numbers

Explanation

When you flow text from one page to another, you can add continuation notices on each page containing the text so that your readers will know what page an article either continues on or is continued from. This type of page number is called a *jump-line page number.* Jump-line page numbers change automatically when you rethread or move text, ensuring that your continuation notices are always correct.

To add a jump-line page number:

1 Create a small text frame below the text frame that continues to another page.

2 In the new text frame, type the continuation text you want—for example, "Continued on." (Leave a space after the text to insert the page number.)

3 Choose Type, Insert Special Character, Markers, Next Page Number (for text that jumps to a subsequent page) or Previous Page Number (for text threaded to a previous page).

4 Move the text frame so that it overlaps the text frame that continues to another page, as shown in Exhibit 4-5. When the frames overlap, the continuation code shows the page number where the next threaded text frame is located.

5 Copy the text frame containing the continuation notice. Remember that you have to select the text frame with the Selection tool before copying it.

6 Go to the page containing the text frame with the continued text.

7 Paste the text frame containing the continuation notice above the text frame with the continued text.

8 Change the continuation notice to indicate where the text is continuing from—for example, "Continued from."

9 Move the text frame so that it slightly overlaps the text frame containing the text that continues from the original page.

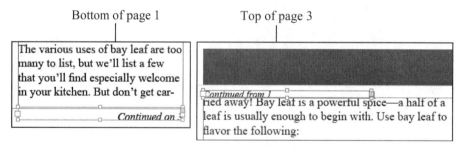

Exhibit 4-5: Continuation notices indicating that text jumps from page 1 to page 3

Do it!

A-3: Adding jump-line page numbers

Here's how	Here's why
1 Go to page 1	At the bottom of the right column, you'll create a continuation notice that tells readers which page the article continues on.
Zoom in on the bottom-right corner of the page	

2 Below the right column of text, create a text frame, as shown

> that you'll find especially welcome in your kitchen. But don't get car-

You'll specify the formatting for the text before you begin typing.

3 Format the text as **Times New Roman**, **11 pt**, **Italic**, and **Align right**

In the Control panel, use the Character and Paragraph Formatting controls.

In the text frame, type **Continued on**

Press `SPACEBAR`

Instead of typing the page number manually, you'll insert a continuation code.

4 Choose **Type**, **Insert Special Character**, **Markers**, **Next Page Number**

5 Click the Selection tool

To select the text frame.

Press `↑` multiple times

> that you'll find especially welcome in your kitchen. But don't get car-
> *Continued on 3*

To move the text frame up until it just overlaps the text frame directly above it, as shown.

When the text frames overlap slightly, the continuation code changes to the number 3 because that page contains the next threaded text frame. You'll also put a "continued from" notice on page 3 so that readers know where the article started.

6 Right-click the **Continued on 3** text frame and choose **Text Frame Options...**

To open the Text Frame Options dialog box.

Under Vertical Justification, from the Align list, select **Bottom**

To align the text to the bottom of the text frame.

Click **OK**

To close the dialog box.

7 Copy the continuation-notice text frame

With the text frame still selected, press Ctrl+C.

8 Go to page 3 and paste the continuation notice on the pasteboard above the page

Press Ctrl+V.

Observe the text frame

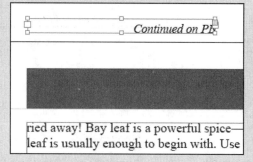

The "3" changes to "PB" to indicate the code behind the marker.

9 In the Control panel, click [≡]

The Align top button.

Change the text alignment to **Align left** and change the type size to **10 pt**

Adjust the position of the frame

So that the text doesn't overlap the green box at the top of the page, but does overlap the story.

10 Select **on** and type **from**

11 Position the text frame as shown

Continued from 3
ried away! Bay leaf is a powerful spice—
leaf is usually enough to begin with. Use

(Position it above the text frame containing the rest of the article from page 1 and overlapping it slightly.) Even though the text frames overlap slightly, the page number does not change. You need to insert a different marker.

12 Select the number **3**

Choose **Type**,
Insert Special Character,
Markers,
Previous Page Number

Continued from 1
ried away! Bay leaf is a powerful spice—
leaf is usually enough to begin with. Use

The code automatically shows the page on which the article originates.

13 Display the entire page in the document window

14 Update and close the document

Topic B: Paragraph formatting

This topic covers the following ACE exam objectives for InDesign CS5.

#	Objective
2.10	Assign and format automatic bullets or numbering for paragraphs.
2.14	Given a feature, avoid widows, orphans, and other typographic problems.

Applying paragraph formatting

Explanation

Any type of formatting that you can apply only to entire paragraphs (rather than to selected characters) is referred to as *paragraph formatting*. Tabs, indents, and keep options are a few examples of format settings that you can apply only to entire paragraphs.

When the Paragraph Formatting controls are active in the Control panel, as shown in Exhibit 4-6, you can change paragraph attributes such as alignment, indent, and drop cap. Paragraph alignment options include Left, Centered, Right, Justified, and Forced. Left and Right alignments create a ragged right or left edge, respectively, while Justified aligns both edges of the text to the margins of the text frame. Centered text is centered relative to the text frame. Forced justification aligns the last line of a paragraph to the right edge of the text frame, whether or not it falls there naturally.

In addition, you can justify text with the last line centered or justify all lines, forcing the last line to stretch across the column. Finally, you can align text toward or away from the spine; this feature comes in handy when you add or remove pages from a layout but want specific text always to align a specific way relative to the spine of your publication.

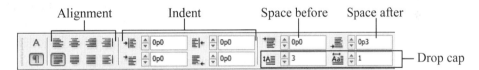

Exhibit 4-6: The Paragraph Formatting controls in the Control panel

Aligning text with tabs

You can use tabs to align text horizontally within single lines or paragraphs. Exhibit 4-7 shows the most commonly used tab types. It is often easiest to type tab characters into the text before setting tabs, so that you can see the results of the tab settings as you set them.

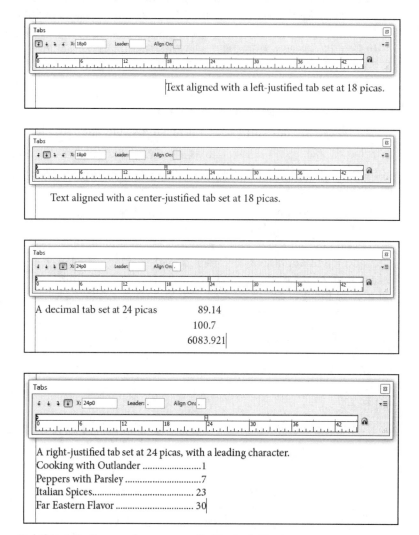

Exhibit 4-7: Some tab types available in InDesign

To set a tab:

1 Use the Type tool to select the paragraph(s) containing the text with tabs.

2 Choose Type, Tabs to open the Tabs panel, shown in Exhibit 4-8. The Tabs panel appears above the text frame, if visible, or above the selected text.

3 Click the tab-alignment button for the tab type you want.

4 Set the tab where you want it by using one of the following methods:

- Click the ruler above the mark where you want the tab to be set. Drag the tab, if necessary, to adjust its position.

- Enter a measurement in the X box.

5 If you want to add a leader to the tab, enter the character you want to use for the leader in the Leader box.

6 When the tab settings are correct, close the Tabs panel.

To change a tab type, select the tab in the Tabs panel and then click the tab-alignment button for a different tab type. To remove a tab, drag the tab mark away from the tab ruler and release the mouse button.

As you're working with the Tabs panel, you can continue to edit text. For example, as you're setting tabs, you can insert or delete tab characters in the text.

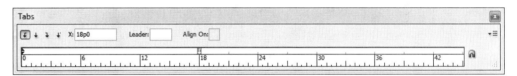

Exhibit 4-8: The Tabs panel

You'll likely work with text that includes data or information typically presented in tables. Although InDesign provides the means to work with tables, you might find it easier to use tabs to align small groups of tabular data, as shown in Exhibit 4-9. If you apply a tab to the first column of data, each line of text must be preceded by a tab character.

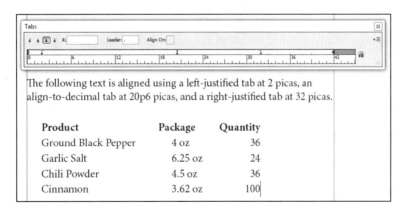

Exhibit 4-9: Text with multiple tabs applied

Do it!

B-1: Setting tabs

The files for this activity are in Student Data folder **Unit 4\Topic B**.

Here's how	Here's why
1 Open Typesetting2 Save the document as **My typesetting2**	
2 Go to page 1	If necessary.
Zoom in on the left side of the page	So that you can see the contents list for the newsletter in the sidebar. The list of articles contains tabs for the page numbers, but they are not spaced correctly.
3 Choose **Type**, **Show Hidden Characters**	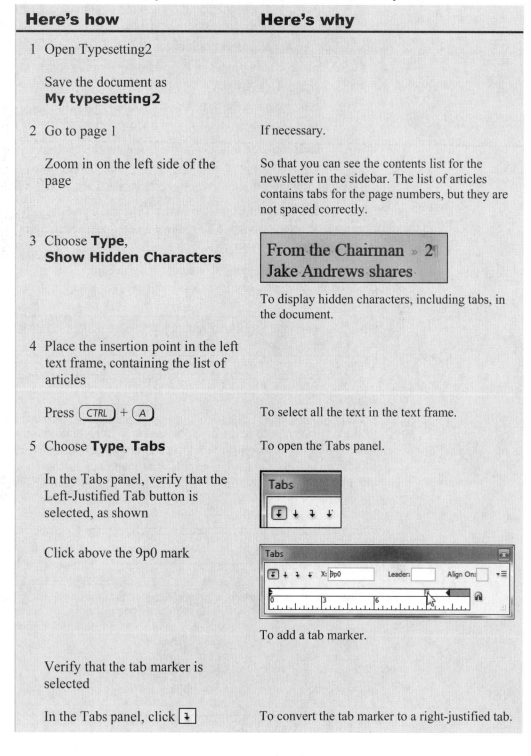 To display hidden characters, including tabs, in the document.
4 Place the insertion point in the left text frame, containing the list of articles	
Press (CTRL) + (A)	To select all the text in the text frame.
5 Choose **Type, Tabs**	To open the Tabs panel.
In the Tabs panel, verify that the Left-Justified Tab button is selected, as shown	
Click above the 9p0 mark	To add a tab marker.
Verify that the tab marker is selected	
In the Tabs panel, click ⬇	To convert the tab marker to a right-justified tab.

6 Drag the tab marker to the right to the 10p3 mark, as shown, and release the mouse button

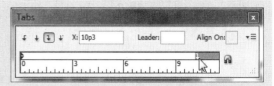

You can view the location of the tab as you drag by observing the X box in the Tabs panel.

Observe the contents list

There is a tab character in the text before each page number, so all the page numbers in the text frame line up with the new tab marker. Now you'll add a dotted leader to connect the article names to the page numbers.

7 On the tab ruler, verify that the tab marker is selected

In the Leader box, type **.**

(Type a period.) To indicate that you want to create a dotted leader (a line of periods) for the selected tab marker.

Press

Dotted leaders appear between the article titles and the page numbers.

8 Close the Tabs panel

9 Deselect the text

Click a blank area of the page.

10 Choose **Type**, **Hide Hidden Characters**

11 Update the document

Indents

Explanation   If text is too close to the left or right edge of a text frame or column, you can use indents to move the text away from those edges in order to improve readability.

In addition, you can use indents to move the beginning of the first line of a paragraph farther to the right, similar to the effect of placing a tab character at the beginning of a paragraph. The advantage of using indents is that when you press Enter after typing a paragraph with an indent, the next paragraph is indented automatically.

To add left or right indents to text:

1   Select the paragraph(s) that you want to indent.

2   Activate the Paragraph Formatting controls in the Control panel, as shown in Exhibit 4-10.

3   Set the indents you want for the text:

- To indent all the text in the selected paragraphs from the left side of the text frame, enter a value in the Left Indent box.

- To indent just the first line of text in each selected paragraph, enter a value in the First Line Left Indent box.

- To indent all text in the selected paragraphs from the right side of the text frame, enter a value in the Right Indent box.

- To indent the right side of the last line of each paragraph to the right, enter a value in the Last Line Right Indent box. You'll also have to insert a right indent tab character and specify a right indent value in order to create this type of indent. This type of indent creates a hanging indent on the right side of the last line of a paragraph.

4   Press Enter to see the effect of the indent settings, and adjust them if necessary.

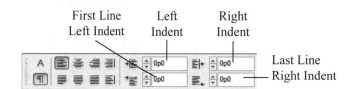

Exhibit 4-10: Indent options in the Control panel

Setting indents by using the Tabs panel

Sometimes you might not know exactly how much you want to indent text. You can also set indents by dragging the indent markers on the ruler that appears above the text when you use the Tabs panel.

To set indents with the Tabs panel:

1   Select the paragraph(s) that you want to indent.

2   Choose Type, Tabs to open the Tabs panel. A ruler appears above the selected text, as shown in Exhibit 4-11.

3   Drag the left, first-line, and right indent markers to where you want them on the ruler.

4   When the indent settings are correct, close the Tabs panel.

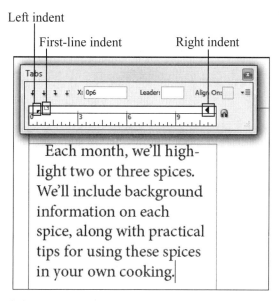

Exhibit 4-11: Indent markers in the Tabs panel

B-2: Creating indents

Here's how	Here's why
1 Go to page 2	You'll indent the callout in the Outlander cookbook article.
2 At the bottom of the middle column, place the insertion point in the paragraph between the two red lines	I love Outlander Cooking! It's simple to use, and it's extremely helpful in making my everyday cooking seem gourmet! —*Ann Salinsky, Thurmont, PA*
3 In the Control panel, click ¶	The Paragraph Formatting Controls button.
In the Control panel, edit the Left Indent box to read **1**	
Edit the Right Indent box to read **1**	1p0 1 0p0 0p0
Press (↵ ENTER)	The text shifts inward on each side.
4 Select the first four paragraphs of the story	Outlander Spices is proud to present our new cookbook for 2009! The cookbook, titled "Outlander Cooking, not only contains hundreds of great recipes, but is also a guide for incorporating our spices into your everyday cooking. Outlander Cooking contains sidebars on special topics, such as "The Best Basils" and "Using Thyme Wisely" together with many lists grouping spices for different uses. The cookbook contains suggestions and recipes for just about every spice we sell. We take those classic dishes you most love and freshen them up with new ingredients and combinations of flavors. Each new idea or technique in the book is accompanied with full color pictures. / and easy-to-follow instructions. Outlander Cooking also contains a large assortment of specialty recipes sent in to us from readers all over the country. / I love Outlander Cooking! It's simple to use, and it's extremely helpful in making my everyday cooking seem gourmet! —*Ann Salinsky, Thurmont, PA* / There are recipes for parsley jelly, salad dressings, and a wide variety of sauces and gravies. For appetizers, there are numerous dips, patés,
	From the beginning of the story to the callout.
5 In the Control panel, edit the First Line Left Indent box to read **1** and press (↵ ENTER)	0p0 0p0 1p0 0p0
	To set the first line of each paragraph to indent 1p.
6 In the Control panel, click ▤	(The "Justify with last line aligned left" button.) To justify the text.
7 Update the document	

Keep options

In multi-page or multi-column documents, you should avoid widows and orphans. A *widow* is the first line of a paragraph that appears as the last line of a column or page. An *orphan* is the last line of a paragraph appearing as the first line of a column or page. Exhibit 4-12 shows an orphan.

In addition, you should ensure that headings or subheadings appear with at least a portion of the paragraph following them in a column or page. You can specify keep options to control widows and orphans and to keep headings or subheadings with the text that follows.

Exhibit 4-12: An orphan

To ensure that a specific number of lines in each paragraph stay together:

1   Use the Type tool to select the paragraph(s) for which you want to avoid widows and orphans.

2   From the Control panel menu, choose Keep Options to open the Keep Options dialog box, shown in Exhibit 4-13.

3   Check Keep Lines Together.

4   Select At Start/End of Paragraph.

5   In the Start box, enter the number of lines that you want to keep together if the beginning of the paragraph is split between columns. In the End box, enter the number of lines that you want to keep together for the end of the paragraph. Entering 2 for this value will eliminate widows and orphans but might result in unbalanced columns.

6   Select an option from the Start Paragraph list (if necessary) to force the paragraph to start at the specified position.

7   Click OK.

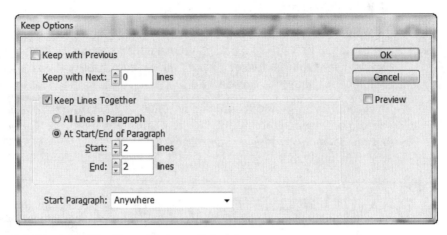

Exhibit 4-13: The Keep Options dialog box

To make sure that a heading stays in the same column or page with at least a portion of the paragraph following it:

1 Use the Type tool to select the heading.

2 From the Control panel menu, choose Keep Options to open the Keep Options dialog box.

3 Check Keep with Previous.

4 In the Keep with Next box, enter a value (up to 5) for the number of lines in the subsequent paragraph that the last line of the current paragraph should stay with.

5 Click OK.

Do it!

B-3:   Setting keep options

Here's how	Here's why
1 On page 2, in the Outlander cookbook story, observe the top of the second column	and easy-to-follow instructions. Outlander Cooking also contains a large assortment of specialty recipes sent in to us from readers all over the country.
	At the top of the second column is an orphan. This is the last line of the paragraph that begins in the previous column.
2 Place the insertion point in the paragraph at the bottom of the first column, as shown	The cookbook contains suggestions and recipes for just about every spice we sell. We take those classic dishes you most love and freshen them up with new ingredients and combinations of flavors. Each new idea or technique in the book is accompanied with full color pictures
3 On the far right side of the Control panel, click ▾≡	The Control panel menu button.
Choose **Keep Options...**	To open the Keep Options dialog box.
4 Check **Keep Lines Together**	

Verify that **At Start/End of Paragraph** is selected	☑ Keep Lines Together
	  ○ All Lines in Paragraph
	  ◉ At Start/End of Paragraph
	      Start: 2 lines
	      End: 2 lines

	To keep only a specified number of lines together, rather than all lines of a paragraph. The default settings will keep the first two and last two lines of a paragraph together, eliminating both widows and orphans.
5 Click **OK**	companied with full color pictures and easy-to-follow instructions. Outlander Cooking also contains a large assortment of specialty recipes sent in to us from readers all over the country.
	The last two lines of the paragraph appear together at the top of the middle column.
6 Update the document	

Bulleted and numbered lists

Explanation

Bulleted and numbered lists typically appear with a *hanging indent*, in which the bullet or number appears to the left of the remaining lines of the paragraph, as shown in Exhibit 4-14. Bulleted and numbered lists use both first-line and left indent settings to position the bullet or number properly in relation to the text.

Method

1. Preheat oven to 425 degrees.
2. In a bowl, mix paprika, caraway seeds, onion flakes, dry mustard, thyme leaves, salt, and ground red pepper.
3. With hands, lightly pat paprika mixture on chicken wings.
4. Brush chicken wings with Buzzard's Best Hot Wing Sauce.
5. Place chicken wings in a large baking dish.
6. Bake 30 minutes or until chicken wings are fork-tender.
7. Place chicken wings on platter. Garnish with celery.

Exhibit 4-14: Numbered list with a hanging indent

To create a bulleted or numbered list from text, first select the paragraphs you want to format as a list. Then click the Bulleted List or Numbered List button in the Control panel. You can adjust the settings for Left Indent and First Line Left Indent in the Control panel.

Numbering across non-threaded frames

You might want to apply numbers to text that appears in different text frames; for example, you might want to use numbers in captions for figures or charts. You can have InDesign number this text automatically.

To apply automatic numbering to text in non-threaded text frames, first create a new numbered-list definition:

1 Choose Type, Bulleted & Numbered Lists, Define Lists to open the Define Lists dialog box.
2 Click New to open the New List dialog box.
3 Edit the List Name box to give your custom list a descriptive name, such as "Non-threaded Numbering."
4 Verify that Continue Numbers Across Stories is checked
5 Click OK to close the New List dialog box.
6 Click OK to close the Define Lists dialog box.

Next, apply the new numbered list to the appropriate text:

1   Select the text to which you want to apply automatic numbering.

2   From the Control panel menu, choose Bullets and Numbering to open the Bullets and Numbering dialog box.

3   From the List Type list, select Numbers.

4   From the List list, select the name you gave the list definition (for example, Non-threaded Numbering).

5   Click OK.

6   For other text that you want to number (in other, non-threaded text frames), repeat steps 1 through 4. Then, from the Mode list, select Continue from Previous Number.

With this method, numbers are applied in sequence. If you remove any frame from the sequence, InDesign updates the other numbers automatically.

Do it!

B-4: Creating bulleted and numbered lists

Here's how	Here's why
1 Go to page 5	The recipe contains lists that should be formatted with bullets and numbers.
2 In the left column, select the text under the heading "Ingredients"	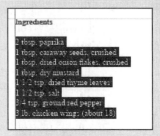
In the Paragraph Formatting Controls section of the Control panel, click	(The Bulleted List button.) To format the select text as a bulleted list.
3 In the right column, select the text under the heading "Method"	
In the Control panel, click ⊞	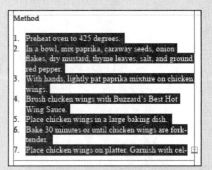
	(The Numbered List button.) To format the selected text as a numbered list. Because some of these paragraphs contain more than one line, InDesign automatically applies a hanging indent. You'll adjust the settings to indent the numbers in the list.
4 In the Control panel, edit the Left Indent box to read **3**	
Edit the First Line Left Indent box to read **-2** and press (↵ ENTER)	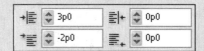
	To adjust the left indent of the numbers and the space between the numbers and the text.
5 Resize the text frame	To show the overset text. Using the Selection tool, double-click the bottom handle of the text frame.
6 Update the document	

Drop caps

Explanation

Drop caps are typographic elements, typically oversized initial letters, which extend down into paragraphs by two or more lines. In InDesign, drop caps are measured both by the number of lines they overlap and by the number of drop cap characters. For example, a drop cap with a setting of three lines extends down into the first three lines in a paragraph. The same setting with four drop cap characters extends the drop caps to the first four characters, as shown in Exhibit 4-15.

Each month, we'll highlight two or three spices. We'll include background information on each spice, along with practical tips for using these spices in your own cooking.

Each month, we'll highlight two or three spices. We'll include background information on each spice, along with practical tips for using these spices in your own cooking.

Exhibit 4-15: Two examples of drop caps

To create a drop cap, place the insertion point in the paragraph where you want the drop cap. Then, in the Control panel, enter a value in the Drop Cap Number of Lines box, as shown in Exhibit 4-16. If necessary, enter a value in the Drop Cap One or More Characters box.

Drop Cap   Drop Cap One or
Number of Lines   More Characters

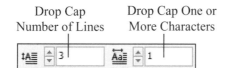

Exhibit 4-16: The drop cap options in the Control panel

Do it!

B-5: Creating drop caps

Here's how	Here's why
1 Go to page 1	You'll create a drop cap in the first paragraph of the story.
2 Place the insertion point in the first paragraph of the "Spices of the month" story	Each month, we'll highlight two or three spices. We'll include background information on each spice, along with practical tips for using these spices in your own cooking. Bay Leaves
3 In the Control panel, edit the Drop Cap Number of Lines box to read **3** and press (↵ ENTER)	To create a drop cap from the first character in the paragraph, as shown in Exhibit 4-16. You can also format additional characters as drop caps.
4 In the Control panel, next to the Drop Cap One or More Characters box, click the up arrow once	‡A≡ ▲▼ 3 Aa≡ ▲ 2
	To format the first two characters as drop caps.
Click the up arrow two more times	**Each** month, we'll highlight two or three spices. We'll include background
	To format the first four characters (the entire first word) of the paragraph as drop caps.
5 Update the document	

Paragraph spacing

Explanation

Adjusting vertical spacing between paragraphs can make the text in a document more readable and engaging, as shown in Exhibit 4-17. Instead of adding an extra return character between paragraphs, you can specify a spacing value.

Bay Leaves

Bay leaves come in many varieties. The popular American variety, laurus nobilis, also known as sweet bay and laurel, is a kitchen staple used widely to flavor meats, soups, stews, gravies, and vegetable dishes. The elliptical leaves are green, glossy, and generally grow to about 3 inches in length.

By themselves, bay leaves are very bitter and hard to chew. Rarely will you find them as the main flavor in a dish. Instead, bay leaves are typically used with other spices to bring flavors together, give depth, and add richness to many types of cooking. You can add them to fish dishes, meats, vegetables, soups, stews, marinades, and sauces, even custards. The key to getting the most out of bay leaves is to always use them sparingly. A little goes a long way!

One of the most flavorful uses for Bay leaves is in the classic herb combination Bouquet Garni, with parsley and thyme. Traditionally, these fresh herbs are tied together, added to a dish, allowed to simmer, and then lifted out at the end of cooking. Dried herbs can be substituted and tied in a bit of cheesecloth. Add other herbs as the nature of the dish and your whims dictate. Try adding lemon, sage, and tarragon with chicken; rosemary and mint with lamb; green peppercorns, orange, and savory to beef. Old, dried leaves tend to lose their flavor, so be sure to replenish your supply often.

Bay Leaves

Bay leaves come in many varieties. The popular American variety, laurus nobilis, also known as sweet bay and laurel, is a kitchen staple used widely to flavor meats, soups, stews, gravies, and vegetable dishes. The elliptical leaves are green, glossy, and generally grow to about 3 inches in length.

By themselves, bay leaves are very bitter and hard to chew. Rarely will you find them as the main flavor in a dish. Instead, bay leaves are typically used with other spices to bring flavors together, give depth, and add richness to many types of cooking. You can add them to fish dishes, meats, vegetables, soups, stews, marinades, and sauces, even custards. The key to getting the most out of bay leaves is to always use them sparingly. A little goes a long way!

One of the most flavorful uses for Bay leaves is in the classic herb combination Bouquet Garni, with parsley and thyme. Traditionally, these fresh herbs are tied together, added to a dish, allowed to simmer, and then lifted out at the end of cooking. Dried herbs can be substituted and tied in a bit of cheesecloth. Add other herbs as the nature of the dish and your whims dictate. Try adding lemon, sage, and tarragon with chicken; rosemary and mint with lamb; green peppercorns, orange, and savory to beef. Old, dried leaves tend to lose their flavor, so be sure to replenish your supply often.

Exhibit 4-17: Text with no space between paragraphs (left), and with paragraph spacing set to 6p (right)

To create vertical space between paragraphs, select the paragraphs for which you want to apply paragraph spacing. Then, in the Control panel, enter values in the Space Before and Space After boxes.

Do it!

B-6: Adjusting space between paragraphs

Here's how	Here's why
1 Select the text **Bay Leaves**, as shown	You'll adjust the spacing before and after this paragraph.
2 In the Control panel, edit the Space Before box to read **p6** and press TAB	
3 Edit the Space After box to read **p3** and press ↵ ENTER	
4 Deselect the text	To see the results.
5 Update the document	

Paragraph rules

Explanation

When you want to add lines above or below type, you should typically use *paragraph rules*. Paragraph rule formatting can apply a line above, below, or overlapping a paragraph. Designers often use a paragraph rule to add a line above or below a heading or subheading.

You can set a paragraph rule's color, width, length, offset, and style. Because rule formatting is applied to a paragraph, if the text re-flows in your document, the rule moves as well, maintaining its position relative to the paragraph to which you applied it. Using a rule generally is better than underlining text, because underlined text uses the same color as the type, with a standard offset, weight, and style that can't be adjusted.

To apply a paragraph rule:

1 Select the paragraph(s) for which you want to apply a paragraph rule.

2 Activate the Paragraph Formatting controls in the Control panel.

3 From the panel menu, choose Paragraph Rules to open the Paragraph Rules dialog box, shown in Exhibit 4-18.

4 From the drop-down list, select either Rule Above or Rule Below.

5 Check Rule On. (Note that Rule Above and Rule Below have separate settings. Check Rule On for both if you want rules both above and below the text.)

6 Set the rule attributes you want.

- In the Weight list, enter a value from 0 pt to 1000 pt. (You will probably use a rule between 0.5 pt and 4 pt with headings or text.)

- From the Type list, select a line style (solid, dashed, dotted, and so on).

- From the Color list, select a color.

- In the Tint box, enter a percentage to tint the color.

- Check Overprint Stroke to prevent the stroke from knocking out underlying inks on a printing press.

- Select a Gap Color and Gap Tint if you have selected any type of line type other than solid.

- From the Width list, select either Column or Text.

- In the Offset box, enter a value to control the rule's vertical offset from the text.

- In the Left Indent and Right Indent boxes, enter values for indenting the rule.

7 Click Preview to see the effect of the settings on the text, and adjust them if necessary.

8 When you're satisfied with the settings, click OK.

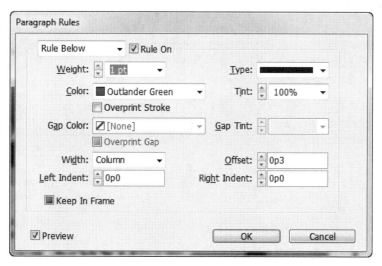

Exhibit 4-18: The Paragraph Rules dialog box

Do it!

B-7: Creating paragraph rules

Here's how	Here's why
1 Select the subheading **Bay Leaves**, as shown	
	You'll create a green rule below the text.
2 From the Control panel menu, choose **Paragraph Rules…**	To open the Paragraph Rules dialog box.
Check **Preview**	To see the changes applied as you make them.
Move the dialog box	So you can see the selected text.
3 From the list at the top of the dialog box, select **Rule Below**	
Check **Rule On**	
	To activate the rule.
4 From the Weight list, select **1 pt**	If necessary.
5 From the Color list, select **Outlander Green**	
6 Edit the Offset box to read **0p3**	
Press (TAB)	
	To apply the setting without closing the dialog box. A green rule appears beneath the text, offset from the baseline by 0p3.
7 Click **OK**	To close the dialog box.
8 Update the document	

Find/Change

Explanation
You might encounter situations in which you want to replace multiple occurrences of a word with another word, or the same word formatted differently. It would be time-consuming to navigate through all the pages of the document and find all occurrences of the word in order to replace it. Instead, you can use the Find/Change dialog box, shown in Exhibit 4-19, to search through the entire document or story.

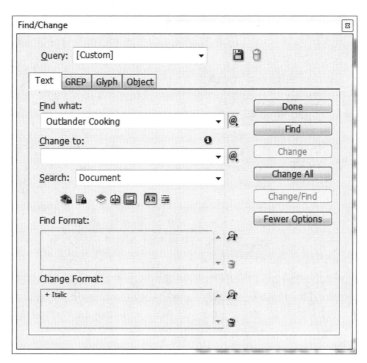

Exhibit 4-19: The Find/Change dialog box

To find or change text:

1 Choose Edit, Find/Change to open the Find/Change dialog box, shown in Exhibit 4-19.

2 In the Find what box, enter the text you want to find.

3 In the Change to box, enter the replacement text.

4 From the Search list, select All Documents to search all open InDesign documents; select Document to search only the active document; select Story to search the text in the selected thread; select To End of Story to search forward in the current thread from the insertion point; or select Selection to search the selected text (if any is selected).

5 Under Find Format, click the "Specify attributes to find" icon to open the Find Format Settings dialog box. From here, select specific formats to find. For example, you can search for text that has a specific font, color, or paragraph format applied.

6 Under Change Format, click the "Specify attributes to change" icon to open the Change Format Settings dialog box. From here, select specific formats to apply to the found text.

7 Click the appropriate icons under the Story list to search in locked layers, locked stories, hidden layers, master pages, or footnotes.

8 Click the Whole Word or Case Sensitive icons as appropriate to limit or expand the search results.

9 Click Find to start the search. Starting at the location of the insertion point, Find/Change will search for text that matches the settings in the Find what section. When an instance is found, it is selected in the document. To start the search from the beginning of the document, deselect all elements on the page and click Find Next.

10 To replace or update a selected instance, click Change, Change All, or Change/Find. If you don't want to apply any changes to an instance, click Find Next to skip the instance and continue the search.

- Clicking Change applies the text and formatting settings in the Change to and Change Format sections to the instance without continuing the search. After you've viewed the changes, click Find Next to continue the search.

- Clicking Change All replaces all instances in the document with the new text and formatting settings. When you use this option, a dialog box appears, stating the number of instances changed.

- Clicking Change/Find applies the text and formatting settings and automatically locates the next instance of the search term.

In addition, you can select an option from the Query list to find and replace common elements, such as replacing straight quotes (") with typographers' quotes ("curly" quotation marks).

Do it!

B-8: Changing formatting by using Find/Change

Here's how	Here's why
1 Deselect all layout objects	You'll search for the term "Outlander Spices" so that you can format it as italics, since it's the title of a book. You want to start at the beginning of the document.
2 Choose **Edit, Find/Change...**	To open the Find/Change dialog box.
3 In the Find what box, enter **Outlander Cooking**	
From the Search list, select **Document**	If necessary.
Click the Case Sensitive button, as shown	

Search: Document ▼

It's possible that the phrase "Outlander cooking" might appear in instances when it is not the book title, in which case you wouldn't want to italicize the phrase.

4 Under Change Format, click	(The "Specify attributes to change" button.) To open the Change Format Settings dialog box.
From the list on the left, select **Basic Character Formats**	
From the Font Style list, select **Italic**	To specify that you want to replace the search term with the same term plus italic formatting.
Click **OK**	To close the dialog box.
5 Observe the Change to box	

Find what:
Outlander Cooking

Change to:
Replace format exists

Search: Document

Done
Find
Change
Change All

An information symbol appears above the text box, indicating that formatting attributes will be changed. The Change Format box shows the type of format changes that will be applied.

6 Click **Find**	Outlander Cookbook .....2 The new edition of Out- lander Cooking is now available. Order yours today!
	Page 1 appears, and the text "Outlander Cooking" is selected in the list of articles.
Click **Change**	To format the text with italics.
7 Click **Find Next**	The document moves to page 2, and another instance of the search term is selected.
Click **Change/Find**	To italicize the text and move to the next instance of the search term.
8 Change each instance of the cookbook title	When you reach the end, a dialog box appears, stating that the search is completed.
Click **OK**	To close the dialog box.
Click **Done**	To close the Find/Change dialog box.
9 Update and close the document	

Topic C: Styles

This topic covers the following ACE exam objective for InDesign CS5.

#	Objective
2.6	Given a scenario, create and apply styles in an automated fashion.

Using styles

Explanation

You can use styles to format characters, paragraphs, and objects quickly and consistently. A *style* is a set of formatting specifications saved under one name. For example, you can create a style that contains specifications such as 24-pt Verdana, bold, and justified alignment. After you create this style, you can apply it to any text in a document.

Paragraph styles

A *paragraph style* is applied to entire paragraphs. It can contain both paragraph formatting and character formatting.

You can create a style based on existing formatting, or you can create a style by entering values for formatting options. To create a paragraph style based on existing formatting:

1 Format a paragraph of text by selecting a font family, size, and alignment.

2 Place the insertion point in the paragraph, or select part or all of it.

3 Activate the Paragraph Styles panel, shown in Exhibit 4-20.

4 Click the "Create new style" button at the bottom of the panel. A new style named Paragraph Style, followed by a number, appears in the list. This style contains the formatting of the selected text.

5 Double-click the style name to open the Paragraph Style Options dialog box so you can edit the style's properties or change its name. When you're done changing settings, click OK.

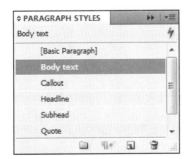

Exhibit 4-20: The Paragraph Styles panel

To create a paragraph style by entering values for the formatting options:

1 From the Paragraph Styles panel menu, choose New Paragraph Style to open the New Paragraph Style dialog box, shown in Exhibit 4-21.

2 Enter a name in the Style Name box.

3 Enter values for any formatting options you want to apply to this style.

4 Check Preview to see these options applied to any selected paragraph.

5 Click OK. The style appears in the list in the Paragraph Styles panel.

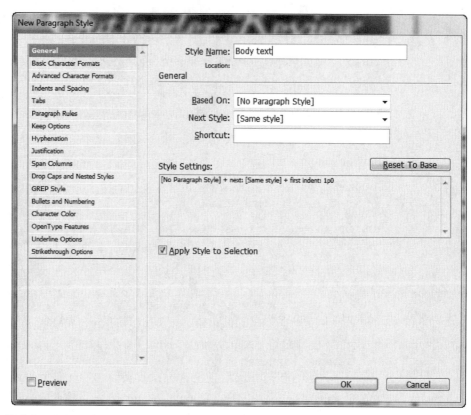

Exhibit 4-21: The New Paragraph Style dialog box

To apply a style to a paragraph, place the insertion point in the paragraph or select a portion of multiple paragraphs. Then, in the Paragraph Styles panel, click the name of the style you want to apply.

Overriding local formatting

When text has a paragraph style applied to it, it is formatted with the attributes defined in the style. But the text can also have additional formatting (for example, if you've italicized a single word in the paragraph). The additional formatting is referred to as a *local override* or *local formatting* and will always take precedence over the style. When you select text that includes local formatting, a plus sign appears next to the style's name in the Paragraph Styles panel. To remove any local formatting in a paragraph, press Alt and click the name of the style you want in the Paragraph Styles panel.

Importing styles

If you or someone else has created a style in an InDesign document, you might want to use that style in another document. Rather than replicating the settings manually, you can import a paragraph style. To do so:

1 From the Paragraph Styles panel menu, choose one of the following:

- Load Paragraph Styles (if you want to load a specific style)
- Load All Text Styles (if you want to load both paragraph and character styles)

2 Select the InDesign document that contains the style or styles you want to import, and click Open.

3 In the Load Styles dialog box, check the styles you want to import and clear those you don't.

4 If a style you're loading has the same name as an existing style, choose an option under Conflict With Existing Style:

- The Use Incoming Definition option replaces the style with the one you're loading, overwriting the attributes and applying them to any text that uses the old style.
- The Auto-Rename option renames the style you're loading, thus keeping both styles.

5 Click OK.

Do it!

C-1: Creating a paragraph style

The files for this activity are in Student Data folder **Unit 4\Topic C**.

Here's how	Here's why
1 Open Typesetting3 Save the document as **My typesetting3**	
2 Go to page 1	If necessary.
3 Place the insertion point in the third paragraph of the story	Bay leaves come in many varieties. The popular American variety, laurus nobilis, also known as sweet bay and laurel, is a kitchen staple used widely to flavor meats, soups, stews, gravies, and vegetable dishes. The elliptical leaves are green, glossy, and generally grow to about 3 inches in length. You'll create a style for all of the body text in the document based on the selected text's formatting.
In the Control panel, edit the First Line Left Indent box to read **1p0** and press (↵ ENTER)	⊹≣ 0p0 ≣⊹ 0p0 ⁺≣ 1p0 ≣⊾ 0p0 To format the paragraph with a 1p0 indent.

4 Open the Paragraph Styles panel

5 Press (ALT) and click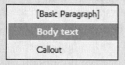

(The "Create new style" button.) To simultaneously create a new style, Paragraph Style 1, and open the Paragraph Style Options dialog box for that style.

Edit the Style Name box to read **Body text**

Check **Apply Style to Selection**

To apply the style you're editing to the text you've selected in the document.

6 In the list on the left, select **Basic Character Formats**, and observe the options

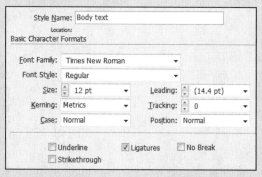

The formatting defaults to that of the selected text.

Click **OK**

7 Observe the Paragraph Styles panel

The selected text now uses the Body text paragraph style.

8 Update the document

Basing styles on other styles

Explanation

To create consistency within a document, you might want to create some styles based on existing styles. That way, you can update several styles at once by updating the style on which they are based. The relationship is similar to the parent/child relationship used with master pages. When you select a style on which to base another style, the formatting for the parent style will be applied to the child style. You can then add additional formatting to the child style.

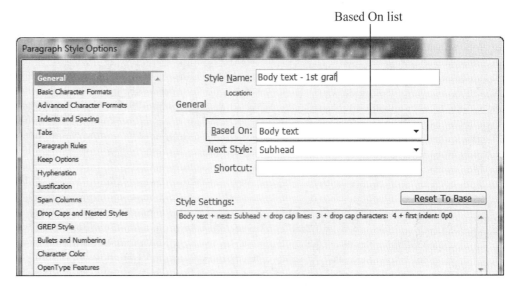

Based On list

Exhibit 4-22: You can base a style on an existing style

To create a style based on an existing style:

1 In the Paragraph Styles panel, either choose New Paragraph Style from the panel menu to open the New Paragraph Style dialog box or double-click an existing style to open the Paragraph Style Options dialog box.

2 For a new style, enter a name for the new style in the Style Name box.

3 From the Based On list, select the parent style, as shown in Exhibit 4-22.

4 Click Basic Character Formats to display the formatting options. Click other formatting sections as necessary.

5 Change formats as needed for the new style.

6 Click OK.

If you want to revert to the original parent style's formatting, click Reset To Base in the Paragraph Style Options dialog box.

Applying styles automatically

Besides basing a style on another style, you can specify the next style to be applied after you press Enter at the end of a paragraph. For example, you might have a headline style; when you press Enter, you might want the next style to be a subhead, followed by an introductory paragraph, followed by body text. You can specify each sequence in the Paragraph Style Options dialog box by selecting a style from the Next Style list.

This method works well for text you're creating in InDesign because pressing Enter automatically applies the style. But you also can use "next styles" for text already in the layout.

To do so, select all of the paragraphs to which you want to apply the parent and child styles. Then, in the Paragraph Styles panel, right-click the parent style and choose "Apply '<style name>' then Next Style."

Do it!

C-2: Creating a style based on an existing style

Here's how	Here's why
1 Place the insertion point in the first paragraph	
2 In the Paragraph Styles panel, click **Body text**	To apply the style, removing the previous formatting. You'll undo this, and then you'll create a style that uses the same formatting as the Body text style but doesn't include the first-line indent and keeps the drop cap.
Choose **Edit**, **Undo Apply Text Style**	
3 In the Paragraph Styles panel, press (ALT) and click 🔽	
4 Edit the Style Name box to read **Body text – 1st graf**	"Graf" is an abbreviation commonly used in journalism. It stands for "paragraph."
From the Based On list, select **Body text**	To specify that you want this style to be a child of the Body text style.
From the Next Style list, select **Subhead**	Based On: Body text Next Style: Subhead
	To specify that you want to apply the style Subhead after a paragraph with the Body text style.
5 In the list on the left, click **Indents and Spacing**	
Edit the First Line Indent box to read **0p0**	
Click **OK**	To close the dialog box and apply the style to the selection.

6 Select the first and second paragraphs

7 In the Paragraph Styles panel, right-click **Body text – 1st graf**

   Choose **Apply "Body text – 1st graf" then Next Style**

To display the shortcut menu.

8 Place the insertion point in the second paragraph

To verify that it uses the Subhead paragraph style.

9 Update the document

Editing styles

Explanation

You might want to edit a style after you've applied it to text in the document. For example, you might want to increase the leading for the body text. To edit a style, display the Paragraph Styles panel menu and choose Style Options to open the Paragraph Style Options dialog box. Change the formatting as needed and click OK. When you edit a style, the changes you make are automatically applied to any text that already uses that style or that uses a style based on it (any child style).

Do it!

C-3: Editing a style

Here's how	Here's why
1 Place the insertion point in the first paragraph	You'll edit the drop-cap formatting and the leading.
2 From the Paragraph Styles panel menu, choose **Style Options...**	
3 In the list on the left, select **Basic Character Formats**	
From the Leading list, select **18 pt**	
4 In the list on the left, select **Drop Caps and Nested Styles**	
Under Drop Caps, edit the Characters box to read **1**	
Click **OK**	To close the dialog box and apply the style changes. The text that uses the style is updated to reflect the changes.
5 Update the document	

Character styles

A *character style* is similar to a paragraph style, with two major differences. First, a character style can contain only character formatting. Second, character styles can be applied to individual characters, whereas paragraph styles uniformly format all text in a paragraph.

As with paragraph styles, it's easiest to define a character style by selecting text that already contains the formatting that you want for the style.

To create a character style:

1   Select the formatted text that you want to use to create a character style.

2   From the Character Styles panel menu, choose New Character Style.

3   In the Style Name box, enter a name for the character style.

4   Click OK.

C-4:   Creating a character style

Here's how	Here's why
1 In the text frame containing the newsletter contents, select **Outlander Cooking**	Outlander Cookbook.....2 The new edition of *Outlander Cooking* is now available. Order yours today!
	You'll format each instance of the term "Outlander Cooking" by using a character style.
Format the text as **Bold Italic**	
2 Open the Swatches panel	
Select **Outlander Green**	
3 Open the Character Styles panel	
Press (ALT) and click [ ]	To open the New Character Style dialog box.
Edit the Style Name box to read **Cookbook title**	
Check **Apply Style to Selection**	
Click **OK**	To close the dialog box and apply the style to the selection.
	Next, you'll use Find/Change to format other occurrences of the phrase.
4 Press (CTRL) + (F)	To open the Find/Change dialog box.
Edit the Find what box to read **Outlander Cooking**	If necessary.

5 Under Change Format, click ⬛	The "Clear specified attributes" button.
From the Search list, select **Document**	(If necessary.) To search the document, instead of just the selected text.
Under Change Format, click ⬛	The "Specify attributes to change" icon.
From the Character Style list, select **Cookbook title**	
Click **OK**	
6 Click **Find**	The first search term InDesign finds is the one you've already formatted.
Click **Find Next**	To find the next instance of the search term.
Click **Change**	To apply the character style.
7 Continue finding and formatting instances of the search term	
Click **Done**	To close the Find/Change dialog box.
8 Update the document	

Style groups

Explanation

By placing styles into groups, you can organize them in folders. You can structure groups into subfolders by nesting groups within groups. You can create groups for character, paragraph, object, table, and cell styles.

To create a style group:

1 In the Styles panel, do one of the following:

- Deselect all styles if you want to create a group at the root level.
- Open an existing group if you want to create a nested group.
- Select the existing styles to include them in a new group.

2 From the Styles Panel menu, choose New Style Group to create a group, or choose New Group from Styles to place the selected styles into a new group.

3 Enter a name for the group and click OK.

Do it!

C-5:   Creating a style group

Here's how	Here's why
1 Deselect all layout objects	
2 Open the Paragraph Styles panel	You'll group the body text styles and the heading styles.
3 Select **Body text – 1st graf** Press (CTRL) and select **Body text**	
4 From the panel menu, choose **New Group from Styles...** Edit the Name box to read **Body text group** Click **OK**	The body text styles are moved under the Body text group folder in the Paragraph Styles panel. You can expand and collapse the styles folder to show and hide the nested paragraph styles.
5 Select the styles **Headline** and **Subhead**	
6 From the panel menu, choose **New Group from Styles...** Edit the Name box to read **Headings group** Click **OK**	
7 Update and close the document	

Unit summary: Typesetting

Topic A   In this topic, you **threaded text** between text frames and added jump-line page numbers.

Topic B   In this topic, you specified **tab** and **indent settings**, created bulleted and numbered lists, controlled text flow by using **keep settings**, adjusted the space between paragraphs, and created and applied **paragraph rules**. In addition, you used **Find/Change** to replace formatting.

Topic C   In this topic, you created, edited, and applied paragraph and character **styles**. You also organized styles into style groups.

Independent practice activity

In this activity, you'll thread text between text frames. You'll also apply some formatting to the text, create paragraph styles, and use Find/Change to change text formatting.

The files for this activity are in Student Data folder **Unit 4\Unit summary**.

1 Open Typesetting practice.

2 Save the document as **My typesetting practice**.

3 On page 1, the text frame in the left column contains overset text. Thread the text frame to the empty text frame in the right column; then continue threading the story into text frames on the remaining pages. (These text frames are already correctly sized and aligned, but they are not linked.) (*Hint:* Make sure frame edges are showing.)

4 Each text frame (except for the next-to-last one) contains some text that should be formatted as a bulleted list. Apply bullet formatting to the list in only one of the frames; then adjust the indent so that the bullets aren't flush with the left edge of the frame.

5 By default, text placed from a Word document is formatted with styles from Word. (Styles from other applications are indicated with a disk icon in the Paragraph Styles panel.) Create a paragraph style for the bulleted list you've formatted; then apply the style to the lists in the remaining text frames.

6 Use the Find/Change command to replace all straight quotes with typographers' quotes. (*Hint:* In the Find/Change dialog box, use the Query list.)

7 Update and close the document.

Review questions

1 You have a layout with guides for three columns. However, in one text frame, you want to use three columns. How can you change the number of columns in a text frame without creating additional frames or changing the layout settings?

A Choose Layout, Margins and Columns.

B Drag to adjust the size of the text frame.

C Select the text frame; then choose Object, Text Frame Options.

D You can't because text frames can contain only a single column.

2 You have three text frames threaded together to display a story. If you delete the second text frame, what happens to the text?

A The text flows into the third text frame.

B The text flows into the third text frame, but any text that was in the second text frame is deleted.

C The text is loaded into the pointer.

D Nothing happens because you can't delete a text frame that's threaded to another frame.

3 You find that your document text contains a number of widows and orphans. Because you're on deadline, you don't want to spend time rewriting to fix the problem. How can you eliminate the widows and orphans?

A Specify settings in the Text Frame Options dialog box.

B Specify settings in the Keep Options dialog box.

C Specify settings in the Paragraph Rules dialog box.

D Specify settings in the Text Wrap panel.

4 Your document contains text that was imported from a word processor. In the past, you've noticed that sometimes quotation marks appear as straight quotes rather than as typographers' quotes. You also want to format only specific phrases with a certain character style you've created. What dialog box can you use to do both of these?

A The Preferences dialog box

B The Text Frame Options dialog box

C The Find/Change dialog box

D The Character Style Options dialog box

5 You've applied a paragraph style to some text. Afterwards, you formatted some words as boldface. How can you override this local formatting?

A Press Alt and click the name of the paragraph style.

B Click the name of the paragraph style.

C From the Paragraph Styles panel menu, choose Style Options.

D Remove all formatting and start over.

6 You want to format only specific words in a paragraph, but the same words are repeated throughout your document. You'd like to be able to format the words wherever they appear, without having to manually apply all of the formats each time. How can you do this?

A InDesign won't let you do this because you can apply styles only to entire paragraphs.

B Insert nonbreaking spaces before and after the text, and then use a paragraph style.

C Use a paragraph style.

D Use a character style.

Unit 5

Modifying items

Unit time: 90 minutes

Complete this unit, and you'll know how to:

A Position text in text frames and format frame edges.

B Place Photoshop images in documents, adjust text wrap, modify graphics, and nest frames.

C Group objects and manipulate objects within a group.

D Create layers and assign objects to them.

Topic A: Text frame options

This topic covers the following ACE exam objective for InDesign CS5.

#	Objective
2.3	Adjust the look of text inside a text frame by using Text Frame Options.

Positioning text within a text frame

Explanation

In addition to positioning text by adjusting leading, paragraph spacing, and left and right indents, you can position text within its text frame. You can vertically align text relative to the text frame, and you can apply a text inset to add space between the text and the frame edge. These techniques are useful when you want to format a text frame, such as by adding a fill color or a stroke around it. By default, frame edges don't have a stroke applied and so are not visible.

To position text in a text frame:

1 Select the text frame and open the Text Frame Options dialog box.

   • Right-click the selected text frame and choose Text Frame Options.

   • Choose Object, Text Frame Options.

2 Click the General tab, if necessary, to display properties for the frame, as shown in Exhibit 5-1.

3 To position the text vertically in the text frame, select an option from the Align list under Vertical Justification. You can select Top, Center, Bottom, or Justify.

4 To inset the text, enter values for Top, Bottom, Left, and Right under Inset Spacing.

5 Click OK.

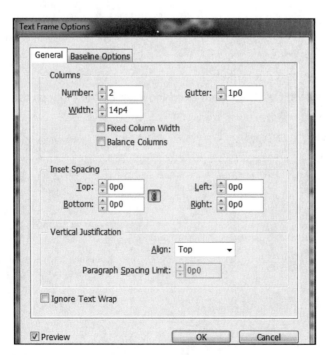

Exhibit 5-1: The General properties in the Text Frame Options dialog box

First Baseline Offset

The baseline is the bottom of a line of text. You can position the first baseline in a text frame so that it is offset from the top of the text frame by a specific amount. This value, called the *first baseline offset*, can be based on various measurements, as described in the table that follows.

Offset	Description
Ascent	(Default) The top of an ascender, as in a lower-case "d," touches the top of the frame, as shown in the first example in Exhibit 5-2.
Cap Height	The top of a capital letter touches the top of the frame.
Leading	The first line's leading value is the distance between the baseline and the top of the frame.
X Height	The height of a lower-case character, such as the letter "x," touches the top of the frame, as shown in the second example in Exhibit 5-2.
Fixed	The distance between the baseline and the top of the frame is set to a specific value.

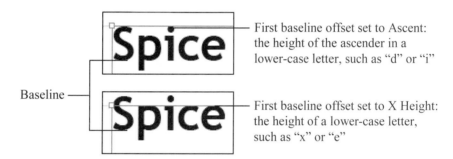

First baseline offset set to Ascent: the height of the ascender in a lower-case letter, such as "d" or "i"

Baseline

First baseline offset set to X Height: the height of a lower-case letter, such as "x" or "e"

Exhibit 5-2: First baseline offsets

You can also specify a minimum distance for the first baseline offset. For example, you can specify an offset of 2p0; the offset will then be at least 2p0, and might be more if one of the character offsets is greater than that amount.

To set the first baseline offset:

1 Select the text frame and open the Text Frame Options dialog box.
2 Click the Baseline Options tab.
3 From the Offset list, select an offset option.
4 In the Min box, set a minimum value, if necessary.
5 Click OK.

Do it!

A-1: Positioning text within a text frame

The files for this activity are in Student Data folder **Unit 5\Topic A**.

Here's how	Here's why
1 Open Modifying items	
Save the document as **My modifying items**	
2 Go to page 1	If necessary.
3 Using the Selection tool, click the text frame containing the list of articles in the left column	The text is flush with the edges of the text frame. You'll inset the text and change the alignment.
Right-click the selected text frame	To display the shortcut menu.
Choose **Text Frame Options...**	To open the Text Frame Options dialog box.
4 Verify that the General tab is active	
5 Under Inset Spacing, edit the Top, Bottom, Left, and Right boxes to read **1p0**	
	To move the text away from the frame edge. Later, you'll format the frame edge with a stroke.
Under Vertical Justification, from the Align list, select **Center**	To center the text vertically in the text frame.
Check **Preview**	(Move the dialog box so you can see the text, if necessary.) To verify the settings.
Click **OK**	To close the dialog box.
6 Update the document	

Formatting frame edges

Explanation

A *frame edge* in InDesign refers to the outer boundaries of a text or graphics frame. By default, frame edges are visible onscreen so that you can work with page items, but they do not print unless you have applied a stroke to them. In documents that contain numerous text or graphics frames, visible frame edges can help to provide a sense of order to the document by indicating the grouping of related items.

To format a frame edge:

1   Select the frame, and then activate the Stroke panel, shown in Exhibit 5-3.
2   From the Weight list, select a stroke weight.
3   From the Type list, select a stroke type.
4   In either the Swatches panel or the Color panel, select a color and shade for the frame.
5   If you've selected a dotted or dashed line style, select a color from the Gap Color list to format the gaps between the dots or dashes.

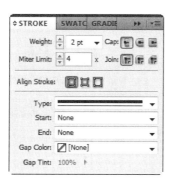

Exhibit 5-3: The Stroke panel

Do it!   **A-2:   Formatting a frame edge**

Here's how	Here's why
1 Select the text frame containing the newsletter contents	(If necessary.) You'll apply a stroke to the edge of the text frame.
2 Press (W)	To switch the screen mode to Preview.
3 Open the Stroke panel	

Weight: 0 pt
Miter Limit: 4 x

To display the stroke options for the text frame. Because the Weight is set to 0 pt, the frame isn't visible.

From the Weight list, select **2 pt**	
From the Type list, select **Thick – Thin**	
4 Activate the Swatches panel	
Click the Stroke icon, as shown	

T
[Paper]

(If necessary.) So that the formatting will apply to the object's stroke, rather than to the fill.

In the Swatches panel, click **Outlander Green**	
Deselect the text frame	To see the results.
5 From the Screen Mode menu, choose **Normal**	
6 Update and close the document	

Topic B: Graphics

This topic covers the following ACE exam objectives for InDesign CS5.

#	Objective
1.3	Given a scenario, work with master pages.
1.8	Modify and transform objects by using the transformation tools and the Control panel.
2.5	Manipulate text flow by using text threading, smart text reflow, resizing, and text wrap.
2.12	Rotate page spreads and, when required, clear the rotation.
4.3	Create a graphic frame that resizes its content automatically.
4.4	Hide or show layers in placed PSD, AI, INDD, and PDF files, and discuss how image transparency is handled.

Modifying graphics

Explanation

You can use graphics as a vital component to reinforce a document's message. In InDesign, there are many ways you can modify graphics to make them more engaging or to fit them within the document's layout the way you want. For example, you can control the way text flows around images, rotate images, add strokes to graphics frames, or anchor images to text. Keep in mind, however, that it's always best to modify graphics in an application such as Photoshop, if possible, because InDesign modifies the way the graphic looks in the document, rather than modifying the graphic itself.

Placing Photoshop files

You can place Photoshop files in InDesign. If you are using Photoshop to generate the graphics for a document, placing the PSD files in your InDesign document can save time because you can view the images in the document without having to *flatten* them first (combining all the layers in the Photoshop file into one layer). You can continue to make updates and changes in Photoshop and see the results directly in the InDesign document.

In InDesign, you can choose to show or hide a particular layer in the Photoshop graphic. To do so, select the graphic and choose Object, Object Layer Options (or right-click the graphic and choose this command from the shortcut menu). In the Object Layer Options dialog box, shown in Exhibit 5-4, click to the left of each layer to turn visibility on or off.

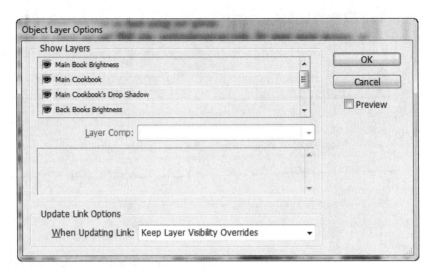

Exhibit 5-4: The Object Layer Options dialog box

Place Photoshop files the same way you place other image formats. If you want to make substantial adjustments to the image, you can do so in Photoshop. When you import a Photoshop file, InDesign maintains a link to the original file so that changes you make in Photoshop are displayed in the document.

Do it!   **B-1:   Placing Photoshop files**

The files for this activity are in Student Data folder **Unit 5\Topic B**.

Here's how	Here's why
1 Open Modifying items2	
Save the document as **My modifying items2**	
2 Go to page 2	
3 Place the Cookbook file	(From the Images folder, which is located in the Common folder.) Cookbook is a Photoshop file.
4 Drag the graphic to the bottom of page 2, as shown	So that it overlaps the Outlander cookbook article and aligns with the top of the text frame and the inside page margin.

Outlander cookbook

Outlander Spices is proud to present our new cookbook for 2009! The cookbook, titled *Outlander Cooking*, not only contains hundreds of great recipes, but is also a guide for incorporating our spices into your everyday cooking.

Outlander Cooking contains sidebars on special topics, such as "The

I love *Outlander Cooking*! It's simple to use, and it's extremely helpful in making my everyday cooking seem gourmet! *—Ann Salinsky, Thurmont, PA*

we sell. We take those classic dishes you most

companied with pictures and ea low instructions. *Outlander* also contains a sortment of recipes sent in t readers all over try.

There are re parsley jelly, sal ings, and a wid of sauces and gr

5 Right-click the graphic	To display the shortcut menu.
Choose **Object Layer Options...**	To open the Object Layer Options dialog box. You'll change which layers of the Photoshop file are visible.
6 To the left of the Back Books Brightness layer, click the eye icon, as shown	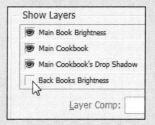

To hide the layer.

7 Check **Preview**	The background cookbooks in the image appear brighter.
Click **OK**	To close the dialog box.
8 Update the document	

Setting text wrap

Text wrap is a frame attribute that causes text behind a frame to flow around it so that the text is not covered. By default, frames do not have a text wrap, so a graphics frame that overlaps text will hide the text.

You can wrap text around any frame by specifying a contour option, which creates a boundary based on a bounding box, automatic edge detection, an alpha channel, a Photoshop path, a graphics frame, or a clipping path. For example, to wrap text around an imported Photoshop image, first save the clipping path in Photoshop. When you place the image in InDesign, select the Apply Photoshop Clipping Path option in the Image Import Options dialog box. When wrapping text around the imported Photoshop image, select the Photoshop Path contour option, which creates a path around the clipping path saved in Photoshop.

To adjust text wrap for a frame:

1 Select the frame.

2 Choose Window, Text Wrap to open the Text Wrap panel, shown in Exhibit 5-5.

3 Click the desired button: No text wrap (default), Wrap around bounding box, Wrap around object shape, Jump object, or Jump to next column.

4 In the Top, Bottom, Left, and Right Offset boxes, enter the distance you want between the graphics frame and the text.

5 If you've selected either "Wrap around bounding box" or "Wrap around object shape," then select an option from the Wrap To list to specify whether to wrap to a specific side or wrap toward or away from the spine.

6 If you are wrapping text around an object shape, select a contour option.

7 Settings take effect immediately. Make adjustments if necessary.

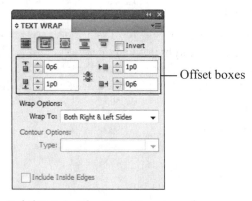

Exhibit 5-5: The Text Wrap panel

Ignoring text wrap

Your layout might have an image to which you've applied text wrap. But you might want some text to appear over a portion of the image, as shown in Exhibit 5-6. To create this effect, you can set the text frame to ignore the text wrap settings of other frames. Here's how:

1   Select the text frame that should ignore text wrap.

2   Choose Object, Text Frame Options.

3   In the Text Frame Options dialog box, check Ignore Text Wrap. Click OK.

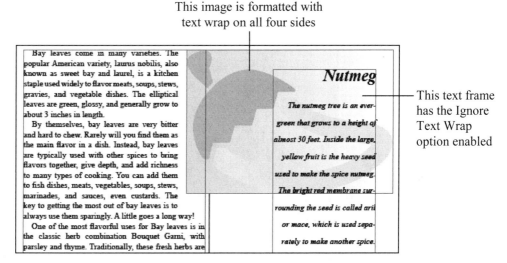

Exhibit 5-6: Using Ignore Text Wrap

Text wrap on master pages

When you place an object on a master page, you might also have text on the master that wraps around the object. But you might not want any text on the document pages to wrap around the object. To apply text wrap on only a master page, first select the object. Then, in the Text Wrap panel, choose Apply to Master Page Only from the panel menu.

Do it!

B-2: Adjusting text wrap

Here's how	Here's why
1 Select the Cookbook graphic	If necessary.
2 Choose **Window, Text Wrap**	To open the Text Wrap panel. You'll apply a text wrap to the selected graphics frame.
3 Click ▣	The "Wrap around bounding box" button.
4 Click ▣	(If necessary.) So that you can set the offsets individually. Because of how the graphic is placed in the layout, you don't need to specify offsets for the top or right edges.
Edit the Left Offset box to read **0p6**	
Edit the Bottom Offset box to read **0p6** and press ⏎ ENTER	
	To apply the settings. The text now wraps around the image.
5 Close the Text Wrap panel	
Update the document	

Panel settings shown: top 0p0, right 0p6, bottom 0p6, left 0p0

Modifying graphics

Explanation

You might want to scale, skew, or flip objects in a document. You can specify dimensions, positioning, and other attributes for frames by using the Control panel, shown in Exhibit 5-7, or by using the Object menu. You can also use some tools to transform objects. In addition to scaling objects by using the Selection tool, you can use the Rotate, Scale, and Free Transform tools.

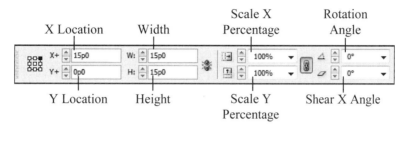

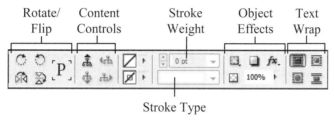

Exhibit 5-7: The Control panel settings for a selected graphics frame

Frame fitting options

You can align graphics to frames by using the Fitting commands. You can adjust a frame or its content so that they fit together correctly; just right-click a graphic, choose Fitting, and then choose Fit Content to Frame, Fit Frame to Content, Center Content, Fit Content Proportionally, or Fill Frame Proportionally.

You can specify a fitting option for placeholder frames so that when a graphic is placed in a frame, the Fitting command is applied. To specify Frame Fitting options:

1 Select a frame.

2 Choose Object, Fitting, Frame Fitting Options.

3 In the Frame Fitting Options dialog box, specify the position (top, bottom, left, right) of the bounding box to use to automatically crop the graphic. Use positive numbers to crop the image, or use negative numbers to add space between the image and the frame.

4 Specify the reference point to be used when graphics are automatically fitted or cropped.

5 From the Fitting list, select Fit Content to Frame, Fit Content Proportionally, or Fill Frame Proportionally.

6 Click OK.

Auto-Fit

Another way to fit graphics to a frame is to use the Auto-Fit feature. Before placing the graphic in a frame, check Auto-Fit in the Control panel. When you place the image, it will automatically be sized to fit the frame.

Rotating frames and graphics

By default, when you use either the Rotate tool or the Control panel to rotate a frame, the contents of the frame rotate as well. For example, if you rotate a graphics frame, the image in the frame rotates in unison with the container. The following list describes various ways to rotate objects:

- To rotate an object by using the mouse pointer, select the object and point to a corner. The mouse pointer changes to a double-headed arrow. Click and drag; as you do, the angle is displayed as a tooltip. Release the mouse button to complete the rotation.
- To rotate an object by using the Control panel, select the object you want to rotate and enter an angle in the Rotation Angle box.
- To rotate an object by using the Rotate dialog box, select the object and choose Object, Transform, Rotate. In the Angle box, enter the angle of rotation for the frame.
- To rotate an object by using the Rotate tool, select the object you want to rotate and select the Rotate tool. The pointer changes to a crosshair. In the Control panel, select a reference point around which to rotate the object. Drag anywhere on the page to rotate the frame. As you drag, the Control panel shows the angle of the frame.

   To rotate the image independently of the graphics frame, select the image with the Direct Selection tool; then use the Rotate tool.

In addition, you can use the Free Transform tool to rotate objects.

Scaling objects

In InDesign, there's an important difference between scaling and resizing. You can scale and/or resize an object's frame, its contents, or both its frame and contents at the same time. Resizing an object changes its width or height values. Scaling changes the width and height values as a percentage of the object's original scale, while also changing the font size, stroke width, and so on.

To resize a frame (and not its contents), use the Selection tool to drag any of the resize handles of an object; or enter values in the Width and Height boxes in the Control panel. To resize a frame's contents (and not the frame), use the Direct Selection tool to select the frame's contents; then either drag the resize handles or enter values in the Width and Height boxes in the Control panel.

There are several ways to scale an object (both the frame and its contents):

- Use the Selection tool to select the object. Then enter values in the Scale X Percentage and Scale Y Percentage boxes in the Control panel.
- Use the Selection tool to select the object. Then hold Ctrl+Shift and drag one of the resize handles.
- Use the Selection tool to select the object. Then select the Scale tool and drag the object's resize handles. Press Shift while dragging to scale the object proportionally. (Holding Ctrl while dragging with the Scale tool scales only the object's frame, not its contents.)

Rotating page spreads

After text is rotated, it can become difficult to read. To compensate for that, you can rotate the page view for a specific page or an entire spread. Start by selected the desired page or spread in the Pages panel. Then, from the Pages panel menu, choose Rotate Spread View and one of the following commands:

- 90° CW
- 90° CCW
- 180°

You can also access the same commands by choosing View, Rotate Spread.

To remove the rotation, select the page or spread in the Pages panel. Display the panel menu and choose Rotate Spread View, Clear Rotation.

Do it!

B-3: Modifying graphics

Here's how	Here's why
1 Select the Cookbook graphic	(If necessary.) You'll scale and resize this graphic so that it fits in a single column.
2 In the Control panel, set the object's reference point to the top-right, as shown	
	When you scale the object, it will scale relative to the top-right corner. This way, you won't have to realign the object to the page guide and the text frame.
In the Control panel, edit the Scale X Percentage box to read **75** and press (TAB)	
	To scale both the X and Y dimensions of the object to 75%. If you've set preferences to Adjust Scaling Percentage, the scale boxes show 75% after you press Enter or Tab. Otherwise, they revert to 100%.
	The object doesn't fit precisely in the column guides, so you'll scale it manually.
3 In the Tools panel, click	(The Scale tool might be hidden under the Free Transform tool.) The Scale tool scales both the frame and its contents simultaneously.
Press and hold (SHIFT)	To scale the graphic proportionally.
Slowly drag the bottom-left corner of the graphics frame up and to the right	
	Until the left edge of the graphics frame aligns with the column guide in the text frame.
4 Go to page 6	The column on the left side of the page contains a rectangle frame. You'll place a photo in the frame and adjust it so that it fits the frame's dimensions.

5 In the left column, use the
   Selection tool to select the empty
   rectangle frame

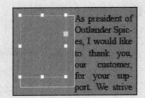

Press (CTRL) + (D)   To open the Place dialog box. Navigate to the
                      Images folder, if necessary.

Double-click **President**   To place the graphic in the frame. Because the
                             graphic is much larger than the frame, you need
                             to scale it to fit.

6 Choose **Object**, **Fitting**,
   Fill Frame Proportionally

To fit the image proportionally. The height now
matches that of the frame, but the image doesn't
fit horizontally and is not centered.

7 Press (CTRL) + (Z) twice   To undo the last two commands and reload the
                              mouse pointer with the President graphic.

In the Control panel, check
Auto-Fit

Point to the empty graphics frame   To place the graphic again. This time it is fitted
and click   to the frame.

8 Point to the graphic   To display the content grabber.

Drag the image to the center

9 Update the document

Nested frames

Explanation

You can use text wrap to flow text around a graphic, but when the text re-flows because you've edited it, the graphic stays in place in the layout. Instead, you might want a particular graphic to appear along with specific text. With text wrap, text flows independently of any graphics, so changes in the text will not automatically affect the graphic's position. But *nesting* a graphics frame within a text frame associates the graphics frame with a particular location in the text itself. A graphics frame nested within a text frame is treated like a text character.

To nest a graphics frame inside a text frame, click to place the insertion point within the text, and then place the graphic. You can also cut and paste a graphic into a text frame. Use the Text Wrap panel to adjust how the graphic interacts with the text around it, and use the paragraph formatting controls to adjust the graphic's position, just as you would with text.

Do it!

B-4: Nesting frames

Here's how	Here's why
1 Go to page 5	You'll create custom bullets for the directions by adding a small graphic to the beginning of each paragraph.
2 Under Method, place the insertion point at the beginning of the first paragraph, as shown	
Place the Small pepper graphic	
	(The Small pepper image is located in the Images folder.) To nest the graphic in the text frame.
Press →	To move the insertion point to after the graphic.
Press TAB	
3 Using the Selection tool, click the graphic	You'll scale it down, and then you'll copy and paste it for the remaining bullets.
4 In the Control panel, edit the Scale X Percentage box to read **50** and press ↵ ENTER	
5 Press ↓ twice	To nudge the graphic down slightly so that it aligns better with the text.

6 Press CTRL + C   To copy the graphic.

Place the insertion point at the   To paste the graphic.
beginning of the next paragraph
and press CTRL + V

Press TAB

Select the graphic and press ↓
twice

7 Continue pasting the graphic at   Remember to press Tab after the graphic and to
the beginning of each of the   nudge the graphic down each time.
remaining paragraphs

8 Place the insertion point in the   You'll format the text so that it has a hanging
text and press CTRL + A   indent.

In the Control panel, edit the Left
Indent box to read **2p0**

Edit the First Line Left Indent box
to read **-2p0**

9 Resize the text frame   So that it fits the overset text.

10 Update and close the document

Topic C: Grouped items

Explanation

When you have multiple items that should always be treated as a unit, you might want to make them a group. Grouping items makes it easier to scale, rotate, and resize items that should be treated as a unit.

The Group command

To group items, select them (press Shift and click each item) and then choose Object, Group. A dashed-line border appears around all the items, indicating that they are grouped, as shown in Exhibit 5-8. When you use the Selection tool to select one of the grouped items, all the items are selected because they act as one unit. To ungroup items, select them and choose Object, Ungroup.

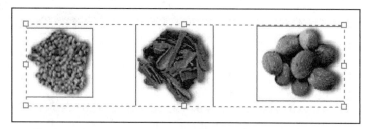

Exhibit 5-8: A border appears around grouped items

Do it!

C-1:   Grouping items

The files for this activity are in Student Data folder **Unit 5\Topic C**.

Here's how	Here's why

1 Open Modifying items3
 	
   Save the document as
   My modifying items3	

2 Go to page 5	(If necessary.) You'll group the objects that make up the small informational box about Stephanie Greene—the reader who provided this month's recipe.

3 Select the picture of Stephanie
   Greene

Press (SHIFT) and click the text
frame below the picture

Press (SHIFT) and click the green
rectangle

4 Choose **Object**, **Group**   To group the objects together.

5 Drag the group to the indicated
   position

6 Update the document

Manipulating items within groups

Explanation

After you've grouped objects, you can make adjustments to them without having to ungroup them. For example, you can reposition items within a group, format frames, and update content. You can use the Direct Selection tool to select an individual object within a group. (Note that clicking a graphics frame with the Direct Selection tool will select the content, not the frame.) You can then adjust that object as you would normally, including replacing pictures and adding text.

If you click a group once with the Selection tool, you select the entire group. If you double-click with the Selection tool, the specific item you clicked in the group is selected.

You can also use the group selection buttons in the Control panel to select elements of a group. To do so:

1 Using the Selection tool, click the group.
2 In the Control panel, click the Select content button.
3 Scroll through the group's contents by clicking the "Select previous object in group" and "Select next object in group" buttons.
4 To select either the contents or the container of a graphics frame, click the "Select content" or "Select container" buttons with the graphics frame selected.

To move an object in a group without first ungrouping all the objects, select the desired object within the group, using the method of your choice. Then drag the object.

Do it!

C-2: Manipulating items within groups

Here's how	Here's why
1 Select the grouped objects	(If necessary.) You'll resize the green rectangle.
2 In the Control panel, click ⊞	(The "Select content" button.) To select the contents of the group. The first object selected is the photo of Stephanie Greene.
Click ⊞▶	(The "Select next object" button.) To select the next object in the group, the green rectangle.
3 Using the Selection tool, drag the frame's bottom handle down to align with the bottom page margin	
4 Click ◀⊞	(The "Select previous object" button.) To select the picture again. You'll adjust its position.
5 Using the Selection tool, point to the graphics frame	Don't point to the center of the image. You will not be using the content grabber.
Drag the graphics frame as shown	
6 Deselect the photo	Click the pasteboard or a blank area of the page.
7 Update and close the document	

Topic D: Layers

This topic covers the following ACE exam objectives for InDesign CS5.

#	Objective
1.6	Use layers to organize the structure of a document.
1.8	Modify and transform objects by using the transformation tools and the Control panel.

Working with layers

Explanation

For most layouts, you'll likely have a combination of text, pictures, and other objects. It can quickly become difficult to manage all of these objects, especially when some objects overlap others. Layers are useful for managing all of the objects in a layout. For example, you can put all of the graphics on one layer and all of the text on another. Then, when you want to edit the text, you can hide the graphics layer. Layers are also useful for hiding and showing objects. For example, to save printer ink, you might hide the graphics layer when printing a draft of a document.

New layers

You create and manipulate layers by using the Layers panel, shown in Exhibit 5-9. Every document contains a default layer, titled Layer 1, which cannot be deleted. To create a layer, click the New Layer button (or hold Alt and click the New Layer button to open the New Layer dialog box). Each additional layer is named with a successive number and is assigned a color, which is used to identify which layer the page items are on.

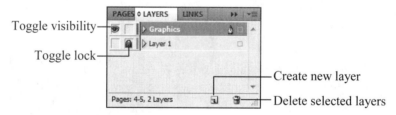

Exhibit 5-9: The Layers panel

You rename a layer by double-clicking it to open the Layer Options dialog box, shown in Exhibit 5-10. Enter a new name for the layer, select options for the layer, and click OK.

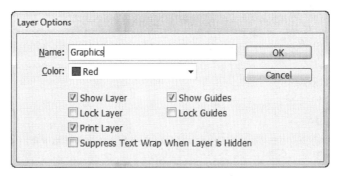

Exhibit 5-10: The Layer Options dialog box

To place new objects on a layer, select the layer you want in the Layers panel and add the objects to the layout as you normally would. Items placed on a layer are outlined with the color corresponding to that layer in the Layers panel. The outline color is shown only when the object is selected.

Duplicating and deleting layers

When you duplicate a layer, you create a copy of all objects on that layer. This result won't be immediately noticeable, however, because InDesign places the copy directly over the original. When you drag an object on a duplicated layer, you will see a copy of the object below it.

To duplicate a layer, do the following:

1 In the Layers panel, select the name of the layer you want to duplicate.

2 From the Layers panel menu, choose Duplicate Layer "<Layer Name>" to create a duplicate layer. The new layer uses the original layer's name with "copy" added after it.

3 Double-click the duplicated layer to open the Layer Options dialog box. Rename the layer, change the layer color, and click OK.

To delete a layer, select it in the Layers panel, and then click the Delete selected layers button or choose Delete Layer "<Layer Name>" from the panel menu. If there are objects on the layer you are deleting, a dialog box will appear, warning you that the layer contains objects.

Hiding and locking layers

You can click a layer's visibility column to hide or show its contents, and click its lock column to lock or unlock the layer. You cannot select or manipulate items on a layer when it is locked. For example, you might lock a layer to prevent yourself from deleting objects accidentally.

Printing layers

To prevent a layer from being printed, clear the Print Layer box when creating the layer. When you print the document, you can specify whether to print hidden or nonprinting layers. For example, you might use a layer to make notes to yourself about the layout, which you wouldn't want to print.

Merging layers and flattening a document

To reduce the number of layers in a document, you can merge layers. When you merge layers, the objects on the layers aren't deleted. Instead, they are transferred to the target layer, and only the layers themselves are deleted.

To merge layers, do the following:

1 In the Layers panel, press Ctrl and click the names of the layers you want to merge.

2 Click the layer that you want to be the target layer. The pen icon next to the layer name indicates which layer is the target layer.

3 From the Layers panel menu, choose Merge Layers to delete the other layers you have selected while keeping the target layer. The objects from the other layers will now appear on the target layer.

When you merge all layers into one, so that only a single layer remains, you have *flattened* the document. To flatten a document by merging all of the layers, select the first layer's name in the Layers panel; then press Shift and click the last layer's name. From the panel menu, choose Merge Layers.

Do it!

D-1: Creating a new layer

The files for this activity are in Student Data folder **Unit 5\Topic D**.

Here's how	Here's why
1 Open Modifying items4	
Save the document as **My modifying items4**	
2 Go to page 4	(If necessary.) It contains objects that fill the page. You want to add a graphic behind the objects to act as a watermark image.
3 Open the Layers panel	
4 Press (ALT) and click ▣	(The Create new layer icon.) To open the New Layer dialog box.
Edit the Name box to read **Graphics**	
Click **OK**	To close the dialog box. The Graphics layer is selected in the Layers panel.
5 In the visibility column, next to Layer 1, click the eye icon	To hide the layer.

6 Place Watermark pepper onto page 4

(The Watermark pepper image is located in the Images folder.) The graphics frame has a red outline, indicating that it is assigned to the Watermark layer. The frame is assigned to the Watermark layer because it was selected in the Layers panel when you imported the graphic.

7 In the Control panel, select the center reference point for the object

Point to the top-left corner as shown

The mouse pointer changes shape, indicating that you can rotate the image. (You can also use the Rotate tool.)

Drag counterclockwise, and rotate the graphic to about **28°**

Use the smart cursor information to set the correct angle.

Release the mouse

To complete the rotation.

8 Using the Selection tool, position the graphic in the center of the page, as shown

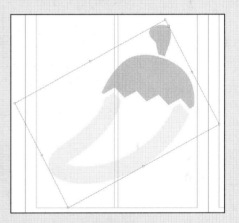

9 Update the document

Layer stacking order

Explanation

Any new layers you add are, by default, placed on top of any previous layers. Any objects you add to a layer will appear above any objects on layers below the current one. To change the layer stacking order, drag a layer up or down in the Layers panel. If you want the objects on a layer always to appear at the bottom of the stacking order, move that layer to the bottom of the list in the Layers panel.

Do it!

D-2:   Changing the layer stacking order

Here's how	Here's why
1 In the Layers panel, to the left of Layer 1, click in the eye column, as shown	Graphics / Layer 1 — To show the default layer again. All items on the page appear, and the watermark image appears on top of the text. You want the image to appear behind the text.
2 In the Layers panel, drag the Graphics layer below Layer 1, as shown	Layer 1 / Graphics — The graphic now appears behind the text.
3 Double-click **Layer 1**	To open the Layer Options dialog box. You'll use this layer for text. When sending a document to a commercial printer, it's a good idea to have all of your text on the top layer.
Edit the Name box to read **Text**	
Click **OK**	
4 Update the document	

Assigning objects to layers

Explanation

You might want to move an object or a group from one layer to another. For example, you might want to move an object from a lower layer to a higher one to make it appear above all other objects in the layout. To do this, select the object in the layout; then, in the Layers panel, drag the dot representing the selected item (shown in Exhibit 5-11) to another layer.

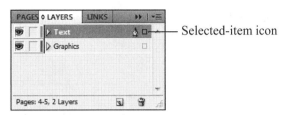

Exhibit 5-11: The Layers panel showing the selected-item icon

D-3: Assigning objects to layers

Here's how	Here's why
1 Go to the master spread A-2-col	You'll add objects on your master pages to layers.
2 Select the banner at the top of the left page	
Press (SHIFT) and select the banner at the top of the right page	
3 In the Layers panel, drag the selected-item icon from the Text layer to the Graphics layer	
	The graphics frames now have red outlines, indicating that they are assigned to the Graphics layer.
4 Select both text frames at the bottom of the page	(The text frames containing the marker for the current page number.) Both of these are already on the Text layer, so you won't move them.
5 Go to the master spread B-3-col	
6 In the Layers panel, hide the Graphics layer	This master is a child of B-3-col. These graphics are "inherited" from the parent master, so they're already on the correct layer.
Show the Graphics layer	
7 Go to the master spread C-Cover 1	
8 Move the top banner and the two rectangles in the left column to the Graphics layer	First, select each object. Then, in the Layers panel, drag the selected-item icon to the Graphics layer.
9 In the Layers panel, click as shown	
	To lock the Graphics layer. You can't select any object on a layer when the layer is locked.
10 Update and close the document	

Unit summary: Modifying items

Topic A   In this topic, you learned how to position text in **text frames** and how to format **graphics frames** so that they have visible edges.

Topic B   In this topic, you learned how to place and manipulate **Photoshop files** in a document. You also learned how to modify graphics and graphics frame containers independently of one another. You then learned how to adjust **text wrap** settings and how to nest frames.

Topic C   In this topic, you learned how to **group** objects and manipulate objects within a group.

Topic D   In this topic, you learned how to create **layers** and assign items to them. You also learned how to change the layer **stacking order** and how to show and hide layers.

Independent practice activity

In this activity, you'll adjust the look of a text frame by modifying the inset. You'll also place a Photoshop file, change which layers are visible, and apply text wrap to the image. Finally, you'll create layers and assign objects to them.

The files for this activity are in Student Data folder **Unit 5\Unit summary**.

1 Open Modifying items practice.

2 Save the document as **My modifying items practice**.

3 Set the top, bottom, left, and right insets of the text frame to **1p0**.

4 Place the Cookbook file, located in the Images folder.

5 For the Cookbook image, hide the Back Books Brightness and Background layers.

6 Apply a text wrap of **0p9** to all sides of the cookbook image. (*Hint:* Choose Wrap Around Object Shape.)

7 Rotate the Cookbook image to about 20°.

8 Arrange the Cookbook image in the layout as shown in Exhibit 5-12.

9 Group the three spice images at the bottom of the page.

10 Create a layer named **Graphics** and rename the default layer as **Text**.

11 Move the graphics to the Graphics layer.

12 Lock the Graphics layer.

13 Update and close the document.

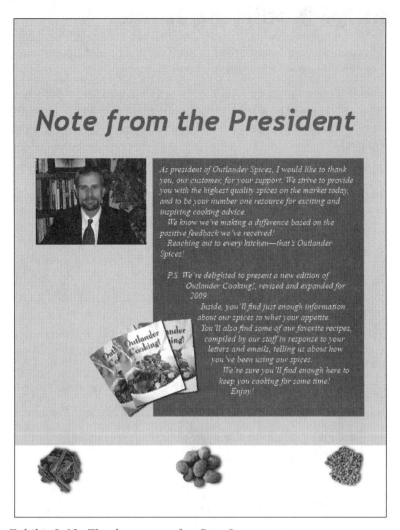

Exhibit 5-12: The document after Step 8

Review questions

1 You want to make the frame edge a 2pt red line. Which two panels or dialog boxes could you use to do this?

A The Text Frame Options dialog box and the Stroke panel

B The Paragraph Styles panel and the Paragraph Rules dialog box

C The Swatches panel and the Effects panel

D The Swatches panel and the Stroke panel

2 After you format the edge of a text frame with a 2pt red stroke, you notice that the text is flush against the stroke. You'd like to add space between the frame edge and the text. How can you do this?

A Change the font size.

B Change the inset spacing in the Text Frame Options dialog box.

C Change the offset in the Paragraph Rules dialog box.

D Apply text wrap to the frame.

3 You've placed a graphic on top of a text frame, and you want the text to flow around the graphic. You should select the graphic and choose:

A Object, Arrange, Send to Back

B Object, Transform, Move

C Window, Layers

D Window, Text Wrap

4 You've imported a Photoshop file that has layers, and you want to turn off one of the layers. You should:

A Return to Photoshop to turn off the layer.

B Choose Window, Layers.

C Choose Object, Clipping Path.

D Choose Object, Object Layer Options.

5 You've placed several objects on a page. When you move one of the objects, you want the others to move with it and stay in the same positions relative to one another. You should select the objects and choose:

A Object, Group

B Object, Lock Position

C Object, Interactive, Move Options

D Object, Text Frame Options

6 Several objects in a layout are grouped together. You want to adjust the position of one of them. How can you select it in order to move it? [Choose all that apply.]

   A Use the Direct Selection tool to drag the object.

   B Use the Selection tool to click the object, and then drag it.

   C Using the Direct Selection tool, press Ctrl and drag the object.

   D Using the Selection tool, double-click to select the object, and then drag it.

7 Your layout contains pages that have many objects that overlap one another. For editing purposes, you want to be able to access the desired objects and hide the ones you don't want right now. What is the best way to do this?

   A Select the objects you want to group together and choose Object, Group.

   B Create a separate master page for those objects that you want to associate with one another.

   C Create new layers and place each overlapping object on a layer, such that overlapping objects are not on the same layer.

   D When you want to edit an object underneath another object, move the topmost object to the pasteboard.

8 After creating layers and placing objects on them, you want to move a particular object to a different layer. First, select the object, and then:

   A Choose Object, Arrange, Bring to Front.

   B In the Layers panel, drag the icon representing the object to the desired layer.

   C From the Layers panel menu, choose Layer Options for "<Layer Name>."

   D In the Layers panel, click the "Delete selected layers" button.

Unit 6

Finalizing documents

Unit time: 45 minutes

Complete this unit, and you'll know how to:

A Print documents, create print presets, and export documents to PDF.

B Prepare documents for commercial printing.

Topic A: Printing and exporting documents

This topic covers the following ACE exam objectives for InDesign CS5.

#	Objective
9.3	Given a scenario, choose the appropriate Print dialog box options.
9.4	Given a scenario, choose the appropriate PDF Preset or PDF Export settings.

Document proofs

Explanation

The main purpose of InDesign is to create documents for print, which can range from a four-color print run at a commercial print shop to several copies on your own laser or inkjet printer. In addition, you might want to generate a copy of a layout as a PDF file so that you can preview and share the publication before it is printed.

The Print dialog box

To print a document on a desktop printer, choose File, Print to open the Print dialog box, shown in Exhibit 6-1. You can select a number of options to customize your print job; for most desktop printing, however, you'll be most concerned with the settings in the General and Setup categories.

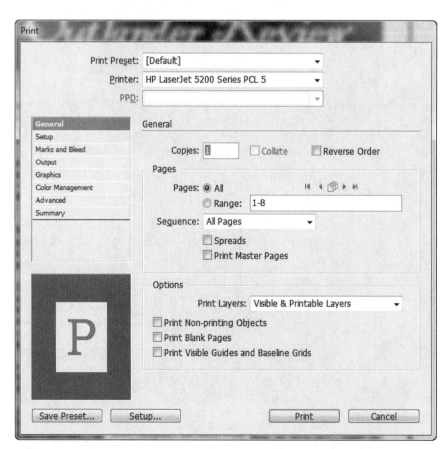

Exhibit 6-1: The Print dialog box with the General options shown

Print presets

After you specify print settings for a document, you can save them so that if you want to print another copy later, you don't need to make the same selections again. To save your print settings, click Save Preset in the lower-left corner of the Print dialog box, name the preset, and click OK. The next time you open and print the document, the settings will be available in the Print Preset list.

To create or edit a print preset:

1   Choose File, Print Presets, Define to open the Print Presets dialog box, shown in Exhibit 6-2. Then do one of the following:

  • Click New to open the New Print Preset dialog box. It looks similar to the Print dialog box shown in Exhibit 6-1.

  • Click the name of an existing Print Preset and then click Edit to open the Edit Print Preset dialog box.

2   Enter a name for the Print Preset and specify the print settings you want.

3   Click OK to save the settings.

4   Click OK to close the Print Presets dialog box.

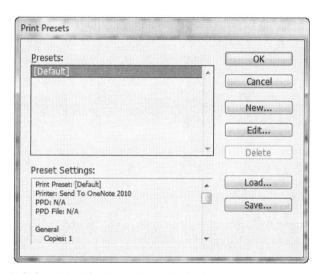

Exhibit 6-2: The Print Presets dialog box

When you want to use a print preset, you can select it from the Print Preset list in the Print dialog box. When you select a print preset, its settings are automatically applied in the Print dialog box.

A-1: Printing a proof

The files for this activity are in Student Data folder **Unit 6\Topic A**.

Here's how	Here's why
1 Open Finalizing1	
Save the document as **My finalizing1**	You'll prepare a document to print as a proof before sending it to a commercial printer.
2 Choose **File**, **Print...**	To open the Print dialog box.
3 From the Printer list, select **HP LaserJet 5200 Series PCL 5**	If necessary.
4 Observe the options under General	Because the newsletter is laid out with facing pages, you'll print an entire spread on one sheet of paper.
Check **Spreads**	Sequence: ▢ ▾ ☑ Spreads ☐ Print Master Pages
	Because you've selected Spreads, you'll set the orientation so that as much of the spread fits on the paper as possible.
5 In the list of categories, click **Setup**	To display the setup options.
For Orientation, click the Landscape button	Orientation: ▢ ▢ ▢ ▢
From the Paper Size list, select **11x17**	To change the paper size; "11x17" is sometimes referred to as "Tabloid."
Under Options, select **Scale To Fit**	To ensure that the spread will fit on a single page.
6 In the list of categories, click **Output**	Because you've selected the HP printer description, the output options show the CMYK color settings. You'll capture these settings as a preset.
7 Click **Save Preset**	(In the bottom-left corner of the dialog box.) To open the Save Preset dialog box.
Edit the Save Preset As box to read **HP Proof**	

8 Click **OK**

Print Pre**s**et: HP Proof

Printer: HP LaserJet 5200 Series PCL 5

To save the preset and close the dialog box. The preset appears in the Print Preset box and will be available the next time you print a document.

9 Click **Cancel**

To close the Print dialog box without printing.

Exporting to PDF

Explanation

Most designers need to share their documents with others. In addition to printing a document, you might also need to e-mail a copy of it to a co-worker or post it online for others to review.

PDF files

A *PDF* (Portable Document Format) file is a universal file format that preserves all the fonts, formatting, graphics, and colors of a publication all in one file. PDF documents provide a flexible way to share and print documents because you can open them on any computer that has Adobe Reader installed, even if the original application or fonts are not installed. PDFs can also have a much smaller file size than the original document, which makes them ideal as e-mail attachments or for uploading to the Web.

To open PDF files, viewers must have Adobe Reader or another application capable of opening PDF documents. Adobe offers a free downloadable version of Adobe Reader on their Web site (www.adobe.com). Also, most Internet browsers now include a plug-in for viewing PDF files online.

Using PDF presets

The presets provided with InDesign will cover most situations in which you need to export an InDesign file as a PDF. When you select a preset, you can change settings as necessary and save them as a new preset.

To export an InDesign file as a PDF:

1 Choose File, Adobe PDF Presets, and choose a preset:

- **High Quality Print** — Suitable for printing on desktop printers.
- **PDF/X-1a:2001** — Widely used standard for professional printing. PDF/X is a standard set of definitions that specify requirements for PDF documents. This preset ensures that your document will print on a professional press.
- **PDF/X-3:2002 and PDF/X-4:2008** — Standard for professional printing that isn't yet as widely adopted as the PDF/X-1a:2001 standard. Use the PDF/X-1a:2001 preset unless your professional printer requests one of these more recent standards.
- **Press Quality** — Suitable for high-quality printing, but not PDF/X-compliant and thus not recommended for professional printing.
- **Smallest File Size** — Creates a compressed PDF, with a smaller file size but lower quality; suitable for e-mail, electronic distribution, or drafts.

2 In the Export dialog box, navigate to and select the location where you want to save the PDF file.

3 In the File name box, enter a name for the PDF file.

4 In the Save as type list, verify that Adobe PDF is selected.

5 Click Save to close the Export dialog box and open the Export Adobe PDF dialog box, shown in Exhibit 6-3.

6 Select an option from the Compatibility list. Some users might not have the most recent version of Adobe Reader installed, so you might want to select an earlier version. However, some more advanced options won't be available for earlier versions.

7 Select options as necessary in the General, Compression, Marks and Bleeds, Output, Advanced, and Security categories. The Summary category lists the options you have chosen.

8 If you have changed any settings and want to save them to use later, click Save Preset. Name the preset and click OK.

9 Click Export to export the PDF.

If you're not sure which specific settings to use, contact your printing vendor and ask how your document should be delivered.

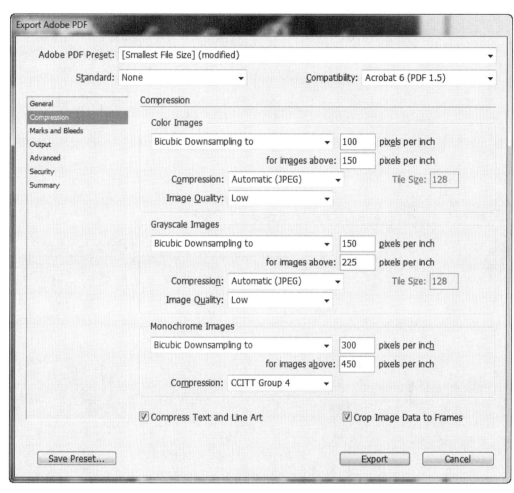

Exhibit 6-3: The Export Adobe PDF dialog box

The following table describes each category in the Export Adobe PDF dialog box.

Category	Used to...
General	Select which pages to print, specify whether to print spreads or single pages, and select other options.
Compression	Select options for dealing with graphics in the document, depending on how you plan to use it and whether you will need high-resolution graphics (for commercial printing) or low-resolution graphics (for Web publishing).
Marks and Bleeds	Specify which printer's marks to include in the PDF file and whether to include bleeds and slug areas.
Output	Set options for color management and the PDF/X setting (if a PDF/X setting has been selected from the Standard list).
Advanced	Set options for embedding font subsets, OPI, transparency flattening, and Job Definition Format (requires Adobe Acrobat Professional).
Security	Specify whether to require passwords for opening the PDF file or for printing and modifying the PDF file.

Do it!

A-2: Exporting to PDF

Here's how	Here's why
1 Choose **File**, **Adobe PDF Presets**, **[Smallest File Size]...**	To open the Export dialog box. You'll create a PDF that you can e-mail to colleagues for review. When sending the document to a commercial printer, however, you should typically use the PDF/X-1a:2001 preset.
From the Save in list, select the current topic folder	If necessary.
Edit the File name box to read **My PDF newsletter**	
Click **Save**	To open the Export Adobe PDF dialog box.
2 Under Pages, verify that **All** is selected	To convert the entire document to a PDF.
Check **Spreads**	
Check **View PDF after Exporting**	To automatically open the PDF after you've exported it.

3 Display the **Compression** options	In the list of categories, click Compression.

Observe the options

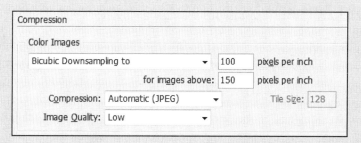

The compression settings generate a much smaller file size, making the PDF easier to e-mail or post online. If you wanted a high-quality printout of the PDF, however, you would need to select higher-image-quality settings and set Compression to None (or select [Press Quality] from the Adobe PDF Preset list).

4 Click **Export**	One or more Warning boxes may appear.
Click **OK**	(If necessary.) To close each warning and convert the document to PDF.
	After a few seconds, the PDF opens in Adobe Reader.
5 Observe the PDF document	There are five pages. Each page contains a spread.
Close Adobe Reader	To return to InDesign.
6 Update and close the document	

Topic B: Preparing for commercial printing

This topic covers the following ACE exam objectives for InDesign CS5.

#	Objective
2.2	Given an option, edit text.
2.8	Create a user dictionary and populate it with custom words.
4.5	Manage placed files by using the Links panel.
9.1	Troubleshoot common printing issues by using Live Preflight.

Preparing documents for printing

Explanation

InDesign documents are often designed with the intent of being sent to a commercial printer. Before you send a project to a commercial printer, however, you need to make sure that the documents are complete and that you're sending everything necessary for the vendor to print the document. Making changes after you've sent your publication to a printer can be very costly.

Checking spelling

As you prepare to send a publication to a commercial printer, it is always a good idea to check for spelling errors. In InDesign, you can check spelling in a particular story or in an entire document.

To check the spelling for a document:

1 Choose Edit, Spelling, Check Spelling to open the Check Spelling dialog box, shown in Exhibit 6-4. The dialog box shows the first suspect word (if the document contains any) in the Not in Dictionary box. If alternative spellings are available in the dictionary, they appear in the Suggested Corrections list beneath the suspect word.

2 Use the dialog box to replace or skip suspected misspellings.

- Enter the correctly spelled word in the Change To box to replace the suspect word and click Change. InDesign replaces the current word with the word you entered and displays the next suspect word. When all the suspect words have been displayed, the dialog box closes.

- Click Skip to proceed to the next suspect word without changing the spelling of the current one.

- Click Ignore All to stop checking this particular word if the spelling is correct and the word recurs in the document.

- Click Change All to change all occurrences of the word to the spelling you have specified.

- Select a spelling from the list of Suggested Corrections and click Change or Change All.

- Click Add to add the current suspect word to the user dictionary. The Add button is active when no words have been selected in the Suggested Corrections list.

- Click Done to stop the spelling check and keep any changes already made.

3   When the spelling check is finished, a green checkmark appears in the dialog box, with the words "Ready to Check Spelling." Click Done to close the dialog box, or click Start to start checking from the beginning.

Exhibit 6-4: The Check Spelling dialog box

Dynamic spelling checking

InDesign can check spelling as you type. To enable this feature, choose Edit, Preferences, Spelling to open the Preferences dialog box with the Spelling options displayed. Check Enable Dynamic Spelling, and then select a color to indicate misspelled, repeated, or uncapitalized words or sentences. When dynamic spelling is enabled, InDesign underlines suspect words. Right-click the word to display a menu; then choose one of the suggested words, open the dictionary, add the word to the dictionary, or tell InDesign to ignore the word.

Autocorrect

By using the Autocorrect feature, you can tell InDesign to automatically correct commonly misspelled words. Choose Edit, Preferences, Autocorrect and check Enable Autocorrect. From the Language list, select the appropriate language. Check Autocorrect Capitalization Errors to have InDesign automatically correct words that should be capitalized. Click Add to add words that you commonly misspell, or select a word from the list and click Remove to have InDesign stop correcting it.

The user dictionary

As you check the spelling in a layout, InDesign might list correctly spelled words as suspect words. For example, many names are not recognized by InDesign and will be identified as suspect words. You could click the Skip button to skip a word, but during future spelling checks, the word will likely be identified as suspect again. To prevent this from happening, you can add words to the default user dictionary or create a new user dictionary to store words you commonly use. When you add a word to a user dictionary, it will no longer be identified as a suspect word during spelling checks.

To create a user dictionary, choose Edit, Preferences, Dictionary to open the Preferences dialog box with the Dictionary options displayed. Under the Language list, click the New User Dictionary button. Navigate to the location where you want to save the dictionary, enter a name for the dictionary, and click Save.

If you want to use an existing user dictionary when checking spelling, click the Add User Dictionary button. Navigate to and select the dictionary, and click Open.

You might have a text document that contains a list of words you want to add to the dictionary. For example, a copyeditor might have compiled a list of uncommon words used in the document and saved it as a text file. Or you might have added words to a user dictionary in another application and then exported that dictionary as a text file. You can import a word list (in a text file) into a dictionary in InDesign.

To import a word list into a user dictionary, first make sure that the words are separated by a space, tab, or paragraph return. Then do the following:

1 Choose Edit, Spelling, Dictionary to open the Dictionary dialog box.
2 From the Target list, select the user dictionary you want to add the words to. (You cannot add words to the default dictionary.)
3 From the Language list, select the appropriate language.
4 Click Import to open the Import User Dictionary dialog box.
5 Locate and select the text file containing the word list you want to import.
6 Select either Add to Dictionary or Replace Dictionary.
7 Click Open.

Do it!

B-1: Checking spelling

The files for this activity are in Student Data folder **Unit 6\Topic B**.

Here's how	Here's why
1 Open Finalizing2	
Save the document as **My finalizing2**	You'll prepare a document to print as a proof before sending it to a commercial printer.
2 Go to page 1	(If necessary.) You'll check for misspelled words in the document. You'll also create a user dictionary to hold words commonly used in Outlander Spices documents.
3 Choose **Edit**, **Preferences**, **Dictionary...**	To open the Preferences dialog box with the Dictionary section active.
4 Below the Language list, click ▣	(The New User Dictionary icon.) To open the New User Dictionary dialog box.
Navigate to the current topic folder	If necessary.
Edit the File name box to read **My dictionary**	
Click **Save**	To close the dialog box and create the dictionary.

5 Click **OK**	To close the Preferences dialog box.
6 Place the insertion point at the top of the contents story	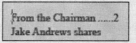
	To start the spelling check at the beginning of the document.
7 Choose **Edit**, **Spelling**, **Check Spelling...**	To open the Check Spelling dialog box.
From the Search list, select **Document**	(If necessary.) To check the whole document.
Click **Start**	InDesign finds the first suspect word. In this case, it's a proper name, and it's spelled correctly. You'll add it to your user dictionary.
8 From the Add to list, select **My dictionary**	
Click **Add**	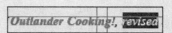
	To add the word to the user dictionary and go to the next suspect word. In this case, InDesign interprets the previous exclamation point as the end of a sentence and suggests that this word should be capitalized, but it is correct the way it is.
9 Click **Skip**	The next word InDesign finds is "emails." You'll edit this word based on InDesign's suggestions.
Under Suggested Corrections, observe the list of words	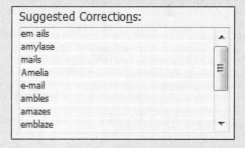
Select **e-mail**	To add this word to the Change To box.
In the Change To box, add an **s** to the end of "e-mail"	
	To make it "e-mails."
Click **Change**	To change the word in the document.
10 Click **Skip**	To go to the next suspect word.
Click **Add**	To add "outlanderspices.com."

11 Continue with the spelling check	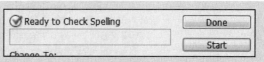
	Until you reach the end of the document. Add, replace, or skip words as necessary. A green checkmark and the words "Ready to Check Spelling" appear in the dialog box when the spelling checker reaches the end of the document.
12 Click **Done**	To close the dialog box.
	While you were checking the spelling, you noticed some text that you want to change. You'll enable the Autocorrect feature to reduce the possibility of more spelling errors.
13 Choose **Edit**, **Preferences**, **Autocorrect...**	To open the Preferences dialog box with the Autocorrect options displayed.
Check **Enable Autocorrect**	A list of commonly misspelled words appears.
Click **OK**	
14 Go to page 7	
In the Spice collection story, select **set**, as shown	**Spice collection** Need a great way to start a collection of spices for either yourself or someone you know? Check out our new Outlander Spice Collection on sale now through the end of the year. The set includes:
Press (DELETE)	
Type **colection** and press (SPACEBAR)	InDesign automatically corrects the misspelled word to "collection."
Press (DELETE)	To delete the extra space.
15 Update the document	

Checking the links for graphics

Explanation

Before you send a publication to a commercial printer, you should check picture links in the document to ensure that all images are accounted for. Graphics placed in InDesign documents are not copied into the document; instead, they are linked to the original file. Therefore, only a screen-resolution preview of the image is stored within the document file. If any graphics links are missing, the publication will print using the screen-resolution versions, which will result in poor-quality images.

The Links panel lists graphics that have been placed in the document. Graphics that have been copied and pasted from other applications, however, will not show up in the Links panel.

To check graphics links and fix any problems in a document:

1 Choose Window, Links to open the Links panel.

2 Scroll through the list of graphics and view the status for each one.

3 Fix any missing or modified graphics. Click a graphics file listed as Missing or Modified to select it.

- To fix a missing link, click the Relink button and navigate to the file's location. Select the folder and click Open.

- To update a modified link, click the Update Link button. InDesign automatically updates the graphic with the modified version.

4 Close the Links panel.

To link an already linked graphic to a new file, select the graphic in the Links panel and click Relink. Navigate to the desired folder, select the new file, and click Open.

B-2: Checking linked graphics

Here's how	Here's why
1 Open the Links panel	To view the list of linked graphics in the document. You'll organize some files before sending them to the printer.
2 Minimize the InDesign application	
3 In Windows Explorer, navigate to the current topic folder	Student Data folder Unit 6\Topic B.
Create a folder titled **My spice images**	
Move **Cinnamon**, **Coriander**, and **Nutmeg** to the My spice images folder	
4 Switch to InDesign	
5 Observe the Links panel	
	The three files you moved now have Missing icons next to them.
6 In the list, select **Cinnamon**	You'll re-establish the link with the file.
Press (CTRL) and click **Coriander** and **Nutmeg**	
	To select all three of the files.

7 Click ⊟	(The Relink button.) To open the Locate dialog box.
Navigate to the **My spice images** folder	
Click **Open**	To re-link the file. A message box appears, stating that InDesign has found and re-linked the other two missing files.
Click **OK**	To close the message box.
8 Update the document	

Checking fonts

Explanation

As you create a publication, you typically place numerous files, each of which might include any number of fonts (even in some graphics files). In addition, you might experiment with various fonts before you settle on the ones you want to use. For this reason, before you send your document to a commercial printer, you should ensure that the document uses only the fonts you intended to use.

To check font usage in a document:

1 Choose Type, Find Font to open the Find Font dialog box.

2 If you want to replace a font with another one, select the font you want to replace in the list.

3 Under Replace With, select a font family and type style from the drop-down lists. Then do one of the following:

  • To replace individual occurrences of the font, click Find First. Click Change to change the font. You can also click Change/Find.

  • To replace all occurrences of the selected font, click Change All.

4 Click Done to close the dialog box.

Do it!

B-3: Checking font usage

Here's how	Here's why
1 Choose **Type**, **Find Font...**	To open the Find Font dialog box and view the list of fonts used in the document. To be consistent, you'll use only Arial, Times New Roman, and Trebuchet in the layout. The Fonts list shows that somewhere in the layout, Calibri was used.
2 In the Fonts in Document list, select **Calibri Regular**	Fonts in Document: Arial Bold Arial Regular Calibri Regular Times New Roman Bold
Click **Find First**	To see where the specified font is used in the document. You'll change it to Arial.
3 Under Replace With, from the Font Family list, select **Arial**	
Click **Change/Find**	There are no more instances of this font in the document. Calibri no longer appears in the Fonts in Document list.
4 Click **Done**	To close the dialog box.
5 Update the document	

Preflighting and packaging

Explanation

In order for a commercial printer to successfully print a publication, they need more than just the project file. Because the commercial printer is outputting the document from a different computer and to a different printing device than those you've used to create the document, it's crucial that they have all the fonts, linked graphics, and setup specifications you've used. Therefore, before you hand a project off to a commercial printer, it's useful to *preflight* the document by checking for problems such as missing links or fonts, low-resolution images, overset text, and other conditions that might affect the quality of the printed document.

Live preflight

As you work in a document, InDesign notifies you of any potential problems by using live preflight. By default, live preflight checks for missing or modified links, overset text, and missing fonts. In the status bar, the Preflight area, shown in Exhibit 6-5, either warns of potential problems or indicates that the document has no errors.

To see information about any errors in the document, double-click the Preflight icon in the status bar to open the Preflight panel, shown in Exhibit 6-6. In the Preflight panel, expand the error categories to see information about the errors and on which pages the errors occur. Click a page-number link on the right to go directly to the corresponding error in the document.

Exhibit 6-5: Live preflight

Exhibit 6-6: The Preflight panel

Preflight profiles

By default, live preflight uses the Basic profile to preflight documents. You can create custom profiles of your own to check for a number of conditions, or you can work with your commercial printer to obtain a profile specific to their requirements. The profile you use could also depend on the specific workflow for your document. For example, you might use one profile for proofing and use another when sending the document to a commercial printer, or you might have different profiles for different printers.

To create a custom profile:

1 Choose Window, Output, Preflight to open the Preflight panel.
2 From the panel menu, choose Define Profiles to open the Preflight Profiles dialog box, shown in Exhibit 6-7.
3 Click the "New preflight profile" icon.
4 Edit the Profile Name box to give the profile a descriptive name.
5 Expand the categories to specify conditions for preflighting a document. Verify that the boxes next to the categories you want to include are checked.
6 Click OK to save the profile.

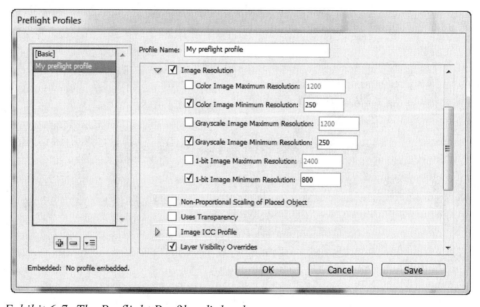

Exhibit 6-7: The Preflight Profiles dialog box

In addition to defining profiles for use on your computer, you can embed profiles in a specific document. That way, when you send the document to someone else, that person can use the same profile to preflight the document. To embed a profile, open the Preflight Profiles dialog box and select the profile you want to embed; then choose Embed Profile from the Preflight profile menu.

Likewise, you can export a profile to share it with others. To do so, choose Export Profile from the Preflight profile menu in the Preflight Profiles dialog box.

Finally, you might receive preflight profiles from colleagues or from your commercial printer. To use them in InDesign, open the Preflight Profiles dialog box. Then choose Load Profile from the Preflight profiles menu.

Do it!

B-4: Preflighting a document

Here's how	Here's why
1 In the status bar, observe the Preflight icon	● 1 error ▼
	There is one error in the document, according to the active preflight profile.
2 Double-click the Preflight icon	To open the Preflight panel.
Expand the TEXT category	To see that the error is overset text.
Expand the Overset text category	To see where in the document the error occurs. It's the text frame on page 6.
Click the page number, as shown	

Error	Page
▽ TEXT (1)	
▽ Overset text (1)	
Text Frame	6

To go to the error in the document.

3 Double-click the bottom resize handle of the text frame	To resize the frame so that there is no overset text.
Observe the Preflight panel	The error no longer appears.
	Your commercial printer has told you that you should use only images with a resolution of at least 250 ppi. In addition, you'll check for images with layer visibility overrides so that you can be sure the correct layers are visible.
4 From the Preflight panel menu, choose **Define Profiles...**	To open the Preflight Profiles dialog box.
5 Click ⊞	(The "New preflight profile" icon.) To begin creating a preflight profile.
Edit the Profile name box to read **My preflight profile**	
6 Expand the IMAGES and OBJECTS category	
Expand the Image Resolution category	
Check **Image Resolution**	To make the category active. When you do, three of the options are checked automatically. You'll use these default settings.

7 Scroll down and check **Layer Visibility Overrides**	

8 Click **OK**	To close the dialog box.
9 In the Preflight panel, in the Profile list, select **My preflight profile**	There are 18 errors in the document.
Expand the IMAGES and OBJECTS category	To see more information about the errors. To fix the errors with image resolution, you would need to obtain higher-resolution images and re-link them.
Expand the "Layer visibility override" section	To see instances of these "errors." You intended to override layers in these images, so they aren't actually errors. You just want to verify that the correct layers are visible.
10 Click **2** as shown	
	To go to the error in the document. InDesign goes to page 2 and zooms to show the image with layer overrides. You could choose Object, Object Layer Options to confirm that the appropriate layers are visible or hidden.
	Next, you'll package the document to send it to a commercial printer.

Packaging a document

Explanation

After you've preflighted a document, you can collect the materials and information needed for commercial printing. InDesign gathers the fonts and linked files used in a document into a folder, along with a copy of the document that you can send to a commercial printer.

To package a document:

1   Choose File, Package to open the Package dialog box.
2   Check for errors in each category.
3   If necessary, close the Package dialog box and fix any errors. (Note that some errors can be fixed in the Package dialog box. For example, you can find and replace fonts, and you can re-link graphics.)
4   Click Package to open the Printing Instructions dialog box.
5   Enter the desired information, and click Continue to open the Package Publication dialog box.
6   In the Folder Name box, enter a name for the package. InDesign will automatically package all elements of the project in this folder.
7   Check options in the Package Publication dialog box. By default, Copy Fonts (Except CJK), Copy Linked Graphics, and Update Graphic Links in Package are checked. Click the Instructions button if you need to change the printing instructions.
8   Click Package, and then click OK to agree to the font use restrictions.

When a document is packaged, InDesign produces the following files and folders:

- **Fonts** — This folder includes the fonts used in the document. Sometimes a font might have the same name but might look different on different machines, affecting the look of your document and the flow of text. Or you might have used a font that your printing vendor doesn't have. Be aware of copyright restrictions when distributing fonts in this way.

- **Links** — This folder contains the original files that your document has links to. The document itself contains only proxies of original files, so it is important to have the originals in order to produce high-quality, high-resolution images in the printed document.

- **Instructions.txt** — This text file contains instructions to the commercial printer. During the packaging process, you can specify what information to include.

- **Original InDesign document** — InDesign includes a copy of the original document.

Do it!

B-5: Packaging a publication

Here's how	Here's why
1 Choose **File**, **Package...**	To open the Package dialog box.
2 Under Package, observe the information	To see information about the fonts, links and images, and colors in the document.

> ⚠️ Links and Images: 27 Links Found; 0 Modified, 0 Missing, 0 Inaccessible
> Images: 0 Embedded, 2 use RGB color space
> Links/Images with Layer Overrides: 4

	A warning symbol appears, indicating that the document includes images that use the RGB color space and that have layer overrides.
3 In the category list, click **Links and Images**	
Check **Show Problems Only**	

> Links and Images
>
> ⚠️ 27 Links Found; 0 Modified, 0 Missing, 0 Inaccessible
> Images: 0 Embedded, 3 use RGB color space
> Links/Images with Layer Overrides: 4
>
> | Name | Type | Page | Status |
> |---|---|---|---|
> | Greene.png | Portab...) RGB | 5 | Linked |
> | President.png | Portab...) RGB | 6 | Linked |
> | Spicy buz...ings.psd | Photoshop RGB | 5 | Linked |

	To see which images use the RGB color space. To correct them, you would need to close the dialog box and re-link them to CMYK images.
4 Click **Package**	A dialog box appears, stating that the publication must be saved to continue
Click **Save**	To save the document. The Printing Instructions dialog box appears. This information will be saved as a text file and packaged with the publication documents for the commercial printer.
5 Click **Continue**	To open the Package Publication dialog box.
Navigate to the current topic folder	InDesign will automatically create a folder containing the publication and related files.
Check **View Report**	

6	Click **Package**	A dialog box appears. Fonts are copyrighted and cannot be freely shared. Commercial printers have extensive font libraries and most likely own the fonts you are using in your layout, so you will click OK. If you are concerned about the legality of sharing the fonts, click Back and clear Copy Fonts (Except CJK).
	Click **OK**	To include the fonts in the package. InDesign packages the document.
7	Observe the Instructions file	The Instructions file automatically opens after InDesign has packaged the publication.
	Close Instructions	
8	In Windows Explorer, navigate to and open **My finalizing2 Folder**	
	Observe the contents of the folder	This folder contains all the files that have been packaged.
9	Switch to InDesign	
10	Close the document	

Unit summary: Finalizing documents

Topic A   In this topic, you learned how to **print** documents, and you created **print presets** to save specific print settings. You also learned how to export documents to **PDF** files.

Topic B   In this topic, you learned how to prepare documents for commercial printing. You learned how to check spelling for a document and how to check the **graphics links** and **fonts** used. You also learned how to **preflight** a document and how to package all the materials needed to send a document to a commercial printer.

Independent practice activity

In this activity, you'll check spelling for a document. You'll also change instances of a specific font and create a PDF version of the document. Finally, you'll preflight and package all materials.

The files for this activity are in Student Data folder **Unit 6\Unit summary**.

1 Open Finalizing practice.

2 Save the document as **My finalizing practice**.

3 Check the spelling for the document.

4 Check the fonts used in the document. Change any font used in the body text so that only Times New Roman is used.

5 Create a PDF version of the document that uses settings favorable for commercial printing.

6 Preflight the document, using the profile you created earlier. (*Hint:* If this profile isn't available, use the embedded Image profile.)

7 Package all the materials for a commercial printer, saving the items in a folder named **My finalizing Practice** within the Unit summary folder. Include all images and fonts, and generate a report. Close the generated report.

8 Close the document. Close InDesign.

Review questions

1 In the Print dialog box, you've specified settings that you want to use when printing your monthly newsletter. How can you save these settings?

A Choose File, Document Presets, Define.

B Choose File, Document Setup.

C In the Print dialog box, click Setup.

D In the Print dialog box, click Save Preset.

2 You want to e-mail a PDF version of your InDesign document to a commercial printer. Which Adobe PDF preset should you choose? [Choose all that apply.]

A High Quality Print

B PDF/X-1a:2001

C Press Quality

D Smallest File Size

3 Your document contains unusual words (such as scientific or technical terms) not typically found in a general dictionary. You want a spelling check to recognize these words as valid. Furthermore, you want to share this list of words with other InDesign users. You should:

A Click Skip in the Check Spelling dialog box.

B Click Add in the Check Spelling dialog box to add the words to the default InDesign dictionary.

C Choose Edit, Preferences, Dictionary and click the Add User Dictionary icon to create a user dictionary.

D Keep a written list of word exemptions that you can pass along to your colleagues.

4 A colleague has compiled a list of unusual words that occur in a document you are working on. She doesn't use InDesign. What's the best way to get those words into your user dictionary?

A You can't. InDesign can't do this.

B Manually enter them into your user dictionary.

C Ask her to export the word list as a text file from the program she is using. Place the document into your InDesign document, run the spelling check, and add each word to the user dictionary.

D Ask her to export the word list as a text file from the program she is using. You can import the word list into your user dictionary.

5 While finalizing your document, you move some images into a separate folder. What should you do next?

A Send an e-mail message to your commercial printer, telling her where to find the images.

B Open the Links panel, select files whose links are missing, and click the Relink button.

C Delete the original images. InDesign automatically saves a copy in the document.

D Nothing. The document is ready to package and send to the commercial printer.

6 You want to make sure that your document doesn't contain any overset text before sending it to a commercial printer. What is the fastest and most reliable way to do this?

A Double-click the Preflight icon to check for errors. By default, the Basic profile includes overset text in the errors it checks for.

B Double-click the Preflight icon to check for errors. Create a profile that checks for overset text.

C Package the publication. InDesign automatically corrects any overset text.

D Scan the document visually to look for overset symbols.

Course summary

This summary contains information to help you bring the course to a successful conclusion. Using this information, you will be able to:

A Use the summary text to reinforce what you've learned in class.

B Determine the next courses in this series (if any), as well as any other resources that might help you continue to learn about InDesign CS5.

Topic A: Course summary

Use the following summary text to reinforce what you've learned in class.

Unit summaries

Unit 1

In this unit, you explored the **InDesign environment** and learned about panels and workspaces. You also learned how to set **preferences**, global and document defaults, and object attributes. In addition, you learned how to use **Adobe Community Help**.

Unit 2

In this unit, you learned how to create a document and a **document preset**. Then you learned how to **create and place text** and apply basic character formatting. You also learned how to place **graphics** in a document. Finally, you learned about the difference between named color swatches and unnamed colors, created custom **color swatches**, and loaded and saved custom swatches.

Unit 3

In this unit, you learned how to position items precisely by using **guides,** the **Control panel**, and smart guides. Then you learned how to create and edit **master pages** and add automatic page numbers to them. You also learned how to apply master pages to existing pages in a document and how to override master-page objects.

Unit 4

In this unit, you **threaded text** between text frames and added jump-line page numbers. Then you specified **tab** and **indent** settings, created bulleted and numbered lists, controlled text flow by using **keep settings**, adjusted paragraph spacing, and created paragraph rules. In addition, you used **Find/Change** to replace formatting. Finally, you worked with paragraph and character **styles**.

Unit 5

In this unit, you learned how to position text in **text frames** and how to format **graphics frames**. Then you learned how to place and manipulate **Photoshop files**, modify graphics and graphics frames independently of one another, set **text wrap**, and nest frames. You also learned how to **group** objects and manipulate objects within a group. Finally, you learned how to work with layers.

Unit 6

In this unit, you learned how to **print** documents, and you created **print presets** to save specific print settings for documents. You also learned how to export documents to **PDF**. Then you learned how to check spelling and how to check the graphics links and fonts used. Finally, you learned how to **preflight** a document and how to **package** all the materials needed to send the document to a commercial printer.

Topic B: Continued learning after class

It is impossible to learn how to use any software effectively in a single day. To get the most out of this class, you should begin working with InDesign CS5 to perform real tasks as soon as possible. We also offer resources for continued learning.

Next courses in this series

This is the first course in this series. The next courses in this series are:

- *InDesign CS5: Advanced, ACE Edition*
- *InDesign CS5: Production, ACE Edition*

Other resources

For more information, visit www.axzopress.com.

Glossary

Baseline

The horizontal position on which a line of type sits. Some lowercase letters—g, j, p, q, and y—extend below the baseline.

Bleed

Any item that extends off the edge of the page to ensure that no white gaps appear between the item and the edge of the paper. The document is then printed on oversized paper. When the paper is trimmed down to size, the bleed item will extend to the edge of the paper.

Character style

A named set of character formats.

Child master

A master page that contains any objects you place on the parent master and that is updated when you update the parent.

Column guides

Nonprinting lines that identify column boundaries.

Desktop publishing

The use of personal computers to produce layouts for print media as well as content for online use and for portable electronic devices.

Document preset

A named collection of settings you save for page size, number of pages, columns, margins, and bleed and slug areas.

Drop cap

A typographic element, typically an oversized initial letter, which extends down into a paragraph by two or more lines.

Facing pages

A pair of pages laid out so that (after printing) one page will be to the left of the binding and the other page will be to the right.

Font

A set of characters, within a font family, with the same size (measured in points), weight (such as Light, Medium, Bold, or Black), and type style (such as Italic); an example is 14pt Palatino Medium Italic.

Font family

A group of fonts, such as Times New Roman, that share similar characteristics and are designed to be used together. Also called a *typeface*.

Frame edges

The outer boundaries of a text or graphics frame.

Gutter

The space between columns.

Hanging indent

A paragraph format in which text below the first line is indented, making it appear to "hang." Hanging indents are often used in bulleted and numbered lists.

Jump-line page number

A continuation notice placed on each page containing text that is flowed from one page to another. The notice indicates which page an article either continues on or is continued from.

Kerning

The horizontal space between a specific pair of characters. The default is zero. Kerning is measured relative to particular fonts, which means that changing fonts will change the kerning proportionally.

Leading

The vertical space allocated to each line of text in a paragraph. Leading is measured in points, and the default setting is Auto. For 12-point type, this is equivalent to 14.4-point leading.

Live preflight

An indication in the status bar that shows whether your document contains any errors that would cause a problem in the production stage.

Local formatting

Additional formatting attributes that you apply to an individual selection in a paragraph that has a paragraph style applied to it. Local formatting overrides paragraph styles.

Margin guides

Nonprinting lines that identify a page's margins.

Master page

A page that serves as a template for pages in a document. Any items on a master page will automatically be added to pages to which the master page is applied.

Master text frame

An option you can select if you want InDesign to automatically insert a text frame that's the size of the area defined by the page margins. The option is in the New Document dialog box.

Nested frame

A frame that's located within a text frame. A graphics frame nested within a text frame is treated like a text character.

N-up views

Options for viewing multiple documents, where N is the number of windows arranged.

Orphan

A paragraph's last line when it appears as the first line of a column or page, while all of the preceding lines in the paragraph are in the previous column or page.

Paragraph formatting

Any type of formatting that you can apply only to entire paragraphs. Tabs, indents, and keep settings are a few examples of paragraph formats.

Paragraph rule

A line above or below a paragraph.

Paragraph style

A named set of formats applied to entire paragraphs and saved in the Paragraph Styles panel. A paragraph style can contain both paragraph formatting and character formatting.

Pasteboard

The area that surrounds the document pages. You can store text and graphics on the pasteboard until you are ready to use them. Items on the pasteboard do not print, but they are saved with the document.

Power zoom

The process of using the Hand tool to zoom in a document by clicking and holding, and then dragging.

Preflight

The process of checking a document for problems such as missing links or fonts, low-resolution images, overset text, and other conditions that might affect the quality of the printed document

Ruler guides

Nonprinting horizontal or vertical lines you use for aid in positioning items. Page guides appear on only a single page; spread guides appear on all pages of a spread and on the pasteboard.

Slug

The area that contains printing and customized color bar information or instructions for printing the document.

Smart guides

Nonprinting guides that provide information about an object's size, location, and alignment with the page and with other objects in the layout.

Spread

Two or more pages that function as a unit. For example, in an opened magazine, the spread consists of the left and right pages.

Story

Text contained in a series of threaded frames.

Style

A named set of formatting specifications.

Text wrap

A frame attribute that causes text behind or in front of a frame to flow around it.

Threading text

The process of flowing text from one frame into additional text frames and then linking the frames so together they form a story.

Tracking

A type of character formatting that tightens or loosens the horizontal spacing of a block of text. Adjusting tracking will not affect any kerning you have applied.

Widow

A paragraph's first line when it appears as the last line of a column or page, while the remaining lines of the paragraph appear in the following column or page.

Index